Pitch like a Pro

Pitch like a Pro

Leo Mazzone and Jim Rosenthal

With a Foreword by Henry Aaron

St. Martin's Griffin ❦ New York

Library of Congress Cataloging-in-Publication Data

Mazzone, Leo.
    Pitch like a pro / Leo Mazzone and Jim Rosenthal.—1st ed.
    p. cm.
    ISBN 0-312-19946-5
    1. Pitching (Baseball). 2. Baseball—Coaching. I. Rosenthal,
Jim. II. Title.
GV871.M39 1999
796.357'22—dc21   98–43623
                                              CIP

Photography by Tom DiPace

Book Design by Bonni Leon Berman

First St. Martin's Griffin Edition: April 1999

10 9 8 7 6 5 4 3 2 1

L.M.—This book is for Bobby Cox

J.R.—This book is dedicated to Murray Rosenthal, my
father, for all his support through the years

Contents

Foreword xi

Acknowledgments xv

When Leo Mazzone first joined the Atlanta Braves as a minor league pitching instructor in 1979, we didn't have anywhere to go but up. We were looking for good people to take us to the next level. I was vice president and director of player development, and believe me, these were lean times for our organization.

There were a few good arms in our farm system: Steve Bedrosian is the one name that comes to my mind. But we were far from having a host of good starters, guys that we could look at and say: "In two or three years these pitchers should be in the big leagues and winning games."

Leo came in and wanted to implement his own program, a simple and practical throwing routine for pitchers that prevented injury and improved performance through repetition. And within a very short time we made substantial progress in the development of our young pitchers.

I've always looked at pitching as a skill that can be perfected through proper instruction. Elite athletes are very much the same in all sports. I've talked with Jack Nicklaus about golf, how he will practice his putting and driving countless times to get the *feel* of the swing. You'd be surprised how similar golf is to baseball when it comes to preparation for success.

I'm a staunch believer that you can do some kind of exercise every single day to prepare for the physical demands of your sport.

Now, of course, Leo has pitched his entire life; he understands what it takes for a pitcher to bounce back from one outing to the next. And based on his experience he has implemented the throwing program here with the Atlanta Braves that you're going to read about in this book.

The throwing program is so simple and yet so imaginative. It dictates that you pitch on a regular basis with a carefully regulated effort. The key is knowing how to throw between starts without going all out on every pitch.

A pitching arm is kind of like an automobile: it has to be prepared for the true test of its ability to perform under pressure. You can't drive a car around at 30 mph for six months and expect it to perform up to par when you take it out on the highway. It's all about realistic preparation, laying the groundwork in the shop for the high-performance requirements of the open road.

Long-term success is the ultimate objective. Leo has our pitchers begin the throwing program in January, and that helps to prevent injuries in spring training.

I can remember from my playing days—and I'm sure this is still a common problem with pitchers today—so many hurlers trying to air it out at 90 mph on the first day of the spring. You know, they probably hadn't picked up a baseball the entire winter. Young kids make this mistake all the time by trying to go all out without proper training or preparation—that's when you're going to get yourself in some serious trouble.

Leo's program is being copied by other teams, and for good reason. It's not just because he's been blessed with great pitchers: Greg Maddux, John Smoltz, Tom Glavine, and Denny Neagle prior to his trade in the winter of '98. Yes, those young men are very gifted. But unlike the rotations of other teams, the Braves' pitchers have been able to pitch—with few exceptions—injury-free and at the peak level of performance. That remarkable run of success is a tribute to our throwing program.

I'm known for my accomplishments as a hitter, not for pitching a baseball. But I do know that building a winning team requires a core of quality pitching.

With a pitcher like Greg Maddux there's a sense of confidence that the team will win—even 1–0—every time out. And a hitter thrives on the belief that one big hit or home run can and will win a ball game.

Injury-free, first-rate performance is nothing new to Leo's pitchers. When I first worked with Leo back in the late seventies and eighties I supervised his implementation of the throwing program in A, AA, and AAA baseball. With the help of the throwing program and a strong grounding in proper mechanics and instruction, our minor league pitchers had almost no arm injuries. This record of health and prosperity reflected the success of the throwing program.

Now, I want to tell you that when Leo first got here a lot of people didn't like his throwing programs. He had to sell the system and prove that it was going to work. It's like anything else in life that's new and different—the initial reaction is always one of skepticism and doubt.

Leo's program, despite its originality and radical departure from the norm, was based on the tried-and-true teachings of Johnny Sain, the pitching legend who worked for the Atlanta Braves as a pitching coach after leading the pitching staffs of the 1961 New York Yankees and 1968 Detroit Tigers to World Series titles.

Sain was the pitching coach on those storied teams, and he worked with great masters such as Whitey Ford and Mickey Lolich.

I've always said that Johnny Sain was two decades ahead of his time, in terms of teaching both how to pitch and how to prepare to pitch—mentally and physically. Leo Mazzone was one of the few pitching coaches of his era who listened and learned from Sain, and a new generation of pitchers will benefit from this collaboration.

Young baseball players today don't listen enough to the guys who have been around and know what it takes to win. When I first came up with the Braves I spent a lot of time just listening to Warren Spahn and Eddie Mathews, the veteran players, talk about baseball. I didn't talk. I just listened!

I want you to pay attention to what Leo has to say about pitching. I'm telling you that this program has been very helpful to pitchers at every level of development in the Braves' organization.

I'm sold on this system because it gives young pitchers the information they need to stay healthy. You can't improve if you can't pitch, and that's the bottom line.

Pitch like a Pro gives you a chance to learn from the coach who has worked with great pitchers like Greg Maddux, Tom Glavine, John Smoltz, and Denny Neagle. I can't say enough about this program and the quality of the instruction you will get in this fine book.

HENRY AARON, *Senior Vice President and Assistant to the President*
Turner Field
Atlanta, Georgia
1998

Acknowledgments

We'd like to thank the following people for helping us with this book: the Atlanta Braves pitching staff, especially Tom Glavine, Greg Maddux, John Smoltz, Denny Neagle, and Mark Wohlers; the Braves media relations department, Glen Serra and Jim Schultz; Tom DiPace, an excellent photographer; George Witte, an excellent editor; Braves hitting instructor Clarence Jones for his insights; and Hank Aaron for believing in this project.

Best wishes to all the coaches and players we've teamed up with at every level of competition, as well as all our family and friends. Special thanks to Whitey Ford and Johnny Sain, in particular, for their inspiration and wisdom.

Chapter 1

The Throwing Program for Pitchers

One of the things about pitching is that a lot of people try to make it a lot more complicated than it really is. My goal in this book is to break everything down for you as simply as possible. Why turn something as basic as throwing a baseball into a science project?

Keeping everything simple and easy to understand is one of the teaching methods I learned from Johnny Sain, a great pitcher in his day and a terrific coach in the sixties, seventies, and eighties.

I worked with Johnny Sain because of his reputation for success—both as a major league pitcher and as a pitching coach with the Yankees, Twins, Tigers, White Sox, and Braves. I came under his wing in 1979; we stayed together in spring training and would go over to his trailer and talk for hours about pitching.

He knew so much about programs for pitching, the nuances of mechanics, and the elements of a winning pitcher. This is not the usual stuff you hear from coaches in the minor leagues—the clichés that give you very little useful information about how to make improvements.

He talked about the need for pitchers to throw a lot between outings. He believed that you need to exercise your arm every day, and his way of exercising the arm was throwing a baseball.

When Sain was at the peak of his career, baseball was locked into the four-man rotation: Quite simply, you would pitch on, say, a Tuesday; take Wednesday off; throw on the side on Thursday—you'd go down to the bullpen and throw off the mound to prepare for your next start—then take Friday off and pitch again on Saturday.

That's how it worked in those days, and Sain had the whole system down to a science. His reputation and his history of coaching 20-game winners, guys who could go to the post all the time, was based on working with healthy pitchers—you have to be healthy to be consistent enough to win 20 games.

So I listened and learned from Sain—he was my guru when it came to understanding the nature of pitching and formulating pitching programs that would enhance performance and protect arms from injuries.

Once I went out on my own as a pitching coach with the Atlanta Braves, I applied what Sain had told me to the reality of baseball in the eighties and nineties—and that meant working within the confines of a five-man rotation. A funny thing happened when the five-man rotation came into vogue: The quality of pitching began to slide a little, and you started to hear about a lot of pitchers getting arm injuries.

I was a minor league pitcher for many years, and I had experience with both the four- and five-man rotation. I always felt that I stayed sharper—and felt better—in a four-man rotation.

The idea behind the five-man rotation was to protect pitchers by giving them an extra day of rest in between starts. In reality, this coddling of pitchers did just the opposite.

A pitching coach has to make adjustments to the reality of the baseball world. My plan was to devise a way to keep our pitchers sharp (as if they were pitching in a four-man rotation) and healthy—the underlying reason for switching to a five-man rotation in the first place.

So here's what I devised to adjust to the five-man rotation: I had our pitchers throw on the extra day off between starts to keep them sharp. I did this on my own. No one knew what I was up to, really. It could have snowballed if anyone had gotten hurt, but quite the opposite happened—the pitchers were healthier and their arms grew stronger.

The pitchers loved it! They threw twice off the mound in between starts. And the guys whom I worked with went to the post consistently for years—there were no sore arms whatsoever. I can't remember having any sore arms, from A ball all the way through my eight years of coaching at the major league level with the Braves.

My reputation grew as a pitching coach who was a teacher and could take care of his pitchers and keep them healthy. This ability to keep pitchers healthy didn't start at the major league level; it's just that the publicity for the throwing program was a product of the success of our young pitching staff at that level.

As Hank Aaron pointed out in the foreword to this book, our pitchers in the minors—the ones who did the extra throwing—stayed healthy the entire time I was a minor league coach with the Braves. But I was on my own; people didn't really know what the heck I was doing. Hank was one of the few baseball people who was both aware of what I was doing and supportive of my methods and objectives.

This phase of my career, working pretty much on my own in the minors, ended in 1986 when Bobby Cox became the general manager of the Braves. We had meetings in Atlanta, where he announced that the new direction for the organization was going to be pitching—rather than hitting—in an effort to turn things around.

The question was: Who was going to take care of the pitchers?

I jumped up, took the floor at the meeting, and began to explain the programs I'd been using with the Braves since 1979 at the minor league level. Bobby liked the programs, and the front office—Hank Aaron, Paul Snyder, and Bobby Dews— backed me up because they knew that our pitchers always went to the post.

There were other pitching coaches at this meeting, and one of them did not agree with my philosophy. He claimed that the pitchers would have nothing left by August if they threw that much.

I asked him, point-blank: "What do you do with your pitchers on the extra day in between starts?" He told me that the pitchers got to play catch in the outfield. I then asked him to explain the difference between playing catch and throwing to a catcher behind the plate.

The problem with my program, according to this coach, was that pitchers would have a tendency to throw too hard if they were pitching off a mound.

My argument was, and is, that it's up to the pitching coach to regulate the effort—that's what we get paid for.

That perspective shot this coach down quite nicely, and my programs became mandatory in the Braves' system from that point onward.

In 1990, I brought those programs to the major league level. The track record here in Atlanta speaks for itself: Our pitchers almost never miss a turn in the rotation, they pitch deeper into games, and they don't get the sore arms and overuse injuries that plague other teams around baseball.

My primary goal as a pitching coach is to ensure that no one misses an appearance—this is true for starters and relievers. I want that goal to extend to anyone trying to learn from what we're doing with the Braves. You can work smarter, not harder, and get better results by following the throwing programs you'll see outlined in this chapter.

Let's Begin with the Throwing Program for Starting Pitchers

Pitch; take a day off; have two mound days, which means you throw off the mound for 10–15 minutes at about 65–75 percent of full velocity; take a day off; and then pitch the next day. And yet it's OK to play catch on those two days off. In other words, I encourage pitchers to throw. I never discourage pitchers from throwing a baseball.

There's one very important thing to understand before embarking on this program: You have to regulate the amount of effort each time you throw between starts. If you pitched as often as Greg Maddux and Tom Glavine and maxed out your between-starts effort—went out and threw at 100 percent effort and at full velocity—then this program would not work.

Pitching is a matter of learning how to put some *feel* and *touch* on the ball. Changing speeds. Command of the fastball.

You can't learn how to pitch if you're playing catch in the outfield, shagging fly balls, and standing around telling jokes and doing nothing.

So when you throw on the side between starts you want to make the ball do something without maxing out your effort. You'd be surprised how much you can learn about pitching—putting touch on the ball and improving the effectiveness of your pitches—when you're not throwing as hard as you can.

The main cause of an arm injury is not a fastball, a slider, a curve, a change, or a split-finger fastball. In fact, I will allow any pitcher to throw any pitch as long as he can throw it properly. Most arm injuries result not from a particular pitch, but from overexertion, "muscling up" (trying to throw too hard in a given situation), or overextension.

Over a period of time, whether you're a starter going deep into a game or a reliever pitching on successive days, you will battle fatigue and try to overcompensate by overthrowing. That's what will hurt you more than anything.

A lot of people will tell you not to throw a split-finger fastball or a slider. When I was coming up as a pitcher through the minors I was told not to throw sliders because they place too much stress on the arm.

Again, the goal is to make adjustments.

Why not teach a young pitcher how to cushion the elbow on a slider to protect his arm?

I remember talking to a pitching coach who said that he had a young pitcher with a great slider, but the organization wouldn't let this phenom throw it for fear he'd get hurt.

My solution in this case would be to show the pitcher how to cushion his elbow on the slider and to call the pitch—quite simply—a short curveball.

A pitcher can throw 10 breaking balls and if you have 10 scouts in the stands five of them will call it a slider and five of them will call it a curve.

The goal is to learn how to master a *quality breaking ball.* I don't care what you call it as long as it's effective.

So when you throw on the side between starts, keep the following objectives in mind:

- Work on command of the fastball.
- Throw as often as possible.
- Throw more often with less exertion.
- Make the ball do something without giving maximum effort.
- Put some touch on your pitches.

Throwing Programs for Little League

Go to the ball field every day. Throw a baseball every day. Coordination will dictate how to throw the pitches and how much you can throw each day.

The key is to be consistent and to throw every day.

Even if you're out on your own, you'd be surprised how much you can learn just by throwing the ball and trying to do different things with your pitches.

In the next chapter, our pitchers with the Braves will show you the proper grips. For now, all I'm asking is that you go to the ballpark every day and throw every day.

Play pickup games with your friends. That's what I did when I was a Little Leaguer, and I learned a lot about the game of baseball.

The main thing for coaches to remember is that it's wrong to clone a delivery with young kids. You let them be as natural as possible and go out and throw a baseball and build up arm strength. Some days they'll be stiffer than others and they won't be able to throw all out.

In a lot of Little Leagues you see kids restricted to throwing six innings per week. I don't think there's anything wrong with having a Little Leaguer throw six innings on Monday and six innings again on Friday.

At the major league level we're throwing a baseball every day. In Little League you do the same darned thing, until it's time to pitch in a Little League game. And even after pitching in a game you can come back and play catch the next day.

Here's an easy-to-follow schedule for Little Leaguers:

Monday Pitch six or seven innings in a game.
Tuesday Play catch, just tossing the ball back and forth without exertion.
Wednesday Get on the mound and practice your pitches.
Thursday Play catch.
Friday Pitch six or seven innings in a game.

Always have the baseball in your hand and always be throwing it. You'd be amazed how a simple thing like playing catch, back and forth, at a young age is a very useful way to build up arm strength and teach yourself about your natural mechanics.

As a rule of thumb you don't want to overexert your arm when you throw the ball back and forth. But you will crank it up a bit to prepare for your next game.

We've had guys here in Atlanta who threw the day before they pitched just to get it going a little bit, just to exercise their arm to prepare to pitch the next day, to rehearse the throwing of the fastball, curve, change, slider. But they're not throwing very hard when they do this; the goal is to practice the craft of pitching to improve arm strength and to get a sense for the touch and feel of the pitches.

You greatly reduce the risk of hurting your arm if you can free yourself up when you throw a baseball. That's the plain truth.

This principle of free-and-easy pitching goes back to what causes arm injuries in the first place: overexertion, overextension, and restricting yourself from start to finish instead of using a free, loose, and easy action.

Before getting into the specific throwing programs for high school and college pitchers, I want to show you a typical throwing regimen for each member of the Braves' starting staff so you can get a sense of how this throw-a-lot mentality pays off with improved endurance and performance.

In the following examples, when I talk about throwing off the mound between starts, I'm referring to a 70 percent of max effort for 10–15 minutes. Part of the 10–15 minutes is spent talking about what's going on with the pitches—criticism, analysis, discussing situations from the last game.

The throwing is supervised and the effort is regulated. That's the key. I want you coaches to encourage your kids to throw—they will love it! And, kids, work to get your coaches on board to ensure that everything goes according to plan.

To give you an understanding of what the throwing program means in a real-world context, I've asked each of our starting pitchers—Tom Glavine, Denny Neagle, John Smoltz, and Greg Maddux—to discuss the benefits of this system for pitchers at all levels of development. You'll find their comments at the end of each individualized workout section.

Tom Glavine

Tom Glavine throws more than any other pitcher on the staff. Check out this sample week of throwing and pitching:

- He pitches on Sunday,
- plays catch in the outfield on Monday,
- pitches from the mound on Tuesday and Wednesday,
- plays catch in the outfield on Thursday, and
- pitches again on Friday.

Tom Glavine on His Program

This is a great program, especially for young pitchers. I would say that 90 percent of all arm injuries, particularly for pitchers at the Little League and high school level, result from a lack of conditioning.

When I look back at my high school career I know for a fact that I didn't throw enough to keep my arm sound and strong. Pitching is like any other skill—you have to practice the skill on a regular basis to improve and to stay in shape.

Many people are scared off by the throwing program because they fear an injury or they just don't understand what throwing on a daily basis really means. The image is of a pitcher throwing as hard as he can all the time—that's not what we're getting at here at all. You have to be smart about how you apply the program to your regular routine.

You have to learn the difference between throwing at 100 percent effort in a game and throwing at 65–70 percent effort when you're throwing on the side between starts. Once you understand what that effort level is, then it becomes much easier to pick up a ball and throw it to the point where you're not punishing yourself because you're throwing it too hard.

The goal is to throw often enough to build up arm strength without going all out. What better way to condition your arm than throwing a baseball on a regular, systematic basis?

Denny Neagle

- He pitches on Sunday,
- takes Monday off,
- pitches from the mound on Tuesday and Wednesday,*
- takes Thursday off, though he will usually play catch, and
- pitches on Friday.

*A variation: Denny pitches Monday, takes Tuesday off, throws from the mound on Wednesday, takes Thursday off, throws from the mound for five minutes on Friday, and then pitches again on Saturday.

Denny Neagle on His Program

The throwing program has been a huge benefit to my career. When I used to pitch for the Pirates I would take a day off after a start and then on the next day I fell into the habit—and this happens to pitchers at all levels—of cranking it out and throwing too hard for too long. Basically, almost anything you do after the first 30 pitches is going to be redundant. You start to get tired, and you don't get as good a workout.

But here with the Braves we throw twice between starts, and a lot of people outside of the organization look at that and think we're throwing too much. But when you minimize your effort at 65–70 percent, putting some feel and touch on the ball, as Leo likes to say, you can fine-tune your control and learn to spot your pitches. The net impact is that you will be sharper with your control.

John Smoltz

- He pitches on Sunday,
- takes Monday off,
- pitches from the mound on Tuesday and Wednesday,
- takes Thursday off, and
- pitches on Friday.

John Smoltz on His Program

The idea of throwing a lot has always made a lot of sense to me. I'm the kind of guy who likes to repeat skills often enough to feel comfortable with them.

Throwing more often with less exertion is very logical. It will make you sharper with your control. I know that some people believe that you only have so many pitches in your arm, but the stress you place on the arm when you pitch is the key factor in health and longevity.

This staff has avoided injuries for three important reasons: the throwing program, emphasis on proper mechanics, and good workout habits. I encourage you to follow our example.

Greg Maddux

- He pitches on Sunday,
- takes Monday off,
- throws on the mound on Tuesday and Wednesday,*
- takes Thursday off, and
- pitches on Friday.

Neagle, Smoltz, and Glavine have the opposite view to many baseball people on this subject: The more pitches they throw, the more comfortable they feel about being ready for the next outing.

Another advantage of this constant reinforcement is that it helps your mental approach. You can focus on how to attack hitters, what you went through in your last game, what you liked or didn't like about the last game. For your coach, it means that he always knows how you feel, mentally and physically, and what you're thinking about your past start and the one to come.

Greg Maddux on His Program

When I pitched with the Cubs I threw once between starts—considerably harder than on the two days I throw between starts with the Braves. Throw more often but with less effort—it makes perfect sense.

It's hard to practice pitching, especially during the season when we're throwing so much as it is. The way Leo has structured this program allows you to get more time to practice your pitches without abusing your arm. The more you practice your pitches, the better you're going to get.

The key to learning how to use this program is being able to trust the benefit of

*A variation: If Maddux feels his pitches are right where he wants them on Tuesday, he'll take Wednesday and Thursday off and come back and pitch on Friday. Mad Dog (Maddux) will pitch *on the side* of the field—off of the mound—either once or twice, depending on how he feels about his pitches.

pitching at 65–70 percent of max. Your whole life you've been led to believe that you have to throw harder to get anything out of it. Put your trust in this program and you will see the benefits of throwing smarter, not harder, with less effort.

Throwing Programs for Relief Pitchers

How many times have you come to the ballpark before a game, maybe to watch batting practice or infield practice, and seen a relief pitcher throwing in the bullpen?

It's a rare sight and I'll tell you why.

The relief pitchers are told—by either the manager or the pitching coach—not to throw because they might pitch that day. These poor guys could go 14 or 15 days without pitching in a game and not throw at all.

My philosophy is that the relievers should get the same amount of attention as the starters. If our relievers do not get into a particular game, the next day I'll have them come over and spin the ball—this includes working on backspin, changing the direction of the spin, changing speeds—for 5–10 minutes. This drill is to prepare for the game that night.

Let me explain the advantages of this system. The main thing is that all the relievers get to throw for the pitching coach on a regular basis. When would a reliever ever work with a pitching coach before a game under typical pregame circumstances?

Hardly ever.

In this program, the one we put to work for the Braves, there's no reason why a reliever can't come over to throw for 5–10 minutes toward the end of batting practice and get to work with the pitching coach and get the same amount of attention as the starters.

In other words, the number 11 man on the pitching staff gets as much attention as the number one guy.

It's all a matter of gaining self-confidence. If you're treated with respect by the coach it helps you mentally and you'll pitch better.

This applies to pitchers at all levels. High school and college coaches need to encourage their athletes to improve. It doesn't happen without hard work, and it's a two-way street—pitchers and coaches have to learn to work together as partners.

Our relief pitchers never go two days in a row without either warming up or throwing off the mound. They'll either pitch in a game, warm up to go into a game, or pitch before the game for 5–10 minutes.

It's especially important to keep the relievers sharp with the Braves, as the starters go so deep into the game. This means the relievers are not getting enough work, which is fine with me. I hope they don't get any work. But I'm going to do everything I can to keep them ready.

Let me give you an example of what I'm talking about from the 1997 National League Championship Series. Alan Embree was warming up during the sixth and final game against the Florida Marlins. Embree hadn't pitched in 11 days; conventional wisdom would dictate that he was not prepared to pitch in such a crucial game. Not true. He hadn't pitched in 11 days, but he'd been on the mound seven out of those 11 days in question.

Throwing a lot, especially for a relief pitcher, can require a period of adjustment. When the Braves trade for a pitcher—starter or reliever—there's a learning curve. But the new guy is always told by our pitchers that the throwing program is the best thing that's ever happened to them—and from that point on the program essentially sells itself.

High School and College Pitchers

In most cases you are probably playing other positions on the days you're not pitching—that fact makes it hard to structure the throwing program according to the Braves' model.

Nevertheless, you still have to prepare for your next start by throwing from the mound between outings. The key is that the effort must be regulated.

One of the great contradictions in baseball is that it's OK for outfielders and infielders to throw every day, but it's a no-no for pitchers.

Why?

First, considerable money is invested in pitchers—a scarce commodity—and second, coaches are afraid of getting fired for being responsible for injuries.

It's ridiculous to baby pitchers like this. In reality, you can actually increase your velocity if you throw often enough to improve arm strength. You can upgrade velocity and develop what I like to call *action balls.* There's life (movement) on the pitch at the end: It sinks, jumps, takes off, rides—whatever. Arm strength improves your ability to throw pitches that have movement.

Arm strength, arm action, and coordination—all of these factors help to improve the velocity of a fastball.

Where a lot of young pitchers mess up is by trying to upgrade velocity by overthrowing. What happens to velocity when you overthrow? It may read the same on a radar gun, but it will be straight as a string and it's in the hitter's wheelhouse.

Throwing Specifics for High School and College Pitchers

A lot of times the star pitcher will also pitch out of the bullpen in critical situations. That throws everything out of whack, but let's construct a basic framework to follow:

- You pitch on Monday,
- play catch or rest on Tuesday,
- throw off the mound on Wednesday,
- play catch or rest on Thursday, and
- pitch again on Friday.

This schedule is consistent with the structure of a four-man rotation.

Now, say your coach wants you to pitch in relief on Thursday after making a start on Monday. You're the number one pitcher on the staff, and Thursday's game is a must-win.

- Pitch on Monday.
- Tuesday off.
- Play catch on Wednesday.
- Pitch in relief on Thursday.

This program has been in effect with the Atlanta Braves at the major league level since June 1990. You've seen the kind of success we've had with it, and yet there's still skepticism from some baseball purists and pitching coaches who fear for their jobs at the expense of developing young pitchers.

I don't think there's a single pitcher on earth who can't benefit from this program. The people who don't believe in the program are guided by a blind fear of overworking pitchers. But this fear is based only on ignorance.

Let me give you another example. At times the Braves will go with a four-man rotation if the schedule allows for it. I've had coaches question that decision because they contend that our pitchers will pile up too many innings. But what if it's the World Series and we need to bring a pitcher back a day early for his next start? What's the difference between doing this during the season and in post-season play?

It's much safer and better to bring a guy back a day early than to set him back a day.

Pitch Counts

I believe in a commonsense pitch count. Maddux may throw 90 pitches and feel the same fatigue that John Smoltz would feel at 125 pitches; it depends on the individual.

Maddux may be done at 110 pitches. Smoltz will usually still have something left past that point. Glavine can usually go further than 100 pitches. Neagle is borderline at 100 pitches.

We have a magic number—about 125 pitches—per start, and that's as far as anyone is going with the Braves. It's usually not a good idea to get into the 140–50 pitch range.

But, of course, there are exceptions to every rule. Smoltz threw 140 pitches in a 2–0 shutout of the Dodgers. Kent Mercker chalked up 133 pitches in tossing a no-hitter against LA in his first start of the 1994 season. That was a rare occasion where a pitcher had a chance to accomplish something special; adrenaline kicked in and took over. That's OK from time to time.

Pitch counts don't mean much to younger pitchers; you don't generally worry about this variable until college. I think at that level you apply the same principles as in pro ball; 125 pitches is as far as you want to go, and you're going to shut a lot of guys down at the 100-pitch mark. Again, it's a personal question.

If you are pitching in Little League or high school and you know you're getting tired, don't be afraid to let your coach in on it. Don't keep it a secret and hurt your team.

It's true that Atlanta Braves pitchers usually don't get close to throwing 125 pitches—even if they go nine innings.

Why?

They can command their fastball and change speeds.

And how do you acquire that skill?

By throwing on the side between outings and learning how to put some touch on the ball.

This is just simple common sense. My goal is to make the process of learning how to pitch as simple and as easy as possible.

If you pick up a baseball every now and then and try to throw it as hard as possible, you won't be able to comb your hair the next day.

But if you pick up a baseball every day and throw it without overexertion, you will be able to bounce back even stronger the next day.

If anyone has doubts about the success of the program, he should consider that our pitchers have only missed a handful of starts in the past seven or eight years. It's a track record of healthy pitching and success—one that I'm quite proud of.

Much of the credit goes to Bobby Cox, one of those rare managers who understands pitching and what his pitchers need to be effective. He does everything he can to protect his pitchers from injury; he will never abuse or overwork his pitching staff—and that's very important.

You can find two types of managers in baseball: The ones who understand pitchers know how to win; the ones who don't understand pitchers are quick to lay blame on the pitching staff for their failures.

On one hand, I've been blessed to work with three managers in the Braves organization who have a tremendous knowledge of pitching: Bobby Dews with Greenville (AA), Jim Beauchamp with Richmond (AAA), and Bobby Cox here in Atlanta. On the other hand, other managers had absolutely no idea what they were doing with the pitching staff—either in the minors or majors—when I worked with them in the seventies and eighties.

You will be forced to deal with all sorts of characters in baseball, good and bad, but it's essential to listen to the people you believe in—the coaches and players who care about you and are trying to help you along on your way to success in this game.

You can always learn by listening, no matter how good you are. I've benefited from my association with the great pitchers of the last 40 years: Johnny Sain, Tommy John, Jim Palmer, Don Sutton, Whitey Ford, and Don Drysdale.

It's no accident that these pitchers were so successful. Intelligence, as much as raw talent, set them apart from the rest.

That's what makes Maddux, Glavine, Smoltz, and Neagle so special—they have the ability to listen and learn from new ideas like the throwing program.

This program, an intangible part of the success of the Braves' pitchers, lays the groundwork for mastering the skills we're going to discuss in the chapters to come—gripping the baseball, how to throw the various pitches, fine-tuning mechanics, and the strategies and tactics that will make you a better pitcher.

Chapter 2

Getting a Grip

Now it's time to focus on throwing the pitches properly. This is a vastly under-rated aspect of pitching; there's so much emphasis on mechanics and so little importance placed on improving the quality of your pitches.

When John Smoltz came over here from the Detroit Tigers he was all messed up; the Tigers had tried to change his mechanics and take him away from what had made him successful in the first place. I'll let Smoltzy fill you in:

> The Tigers' coaches tried to change everything. I thought I was a pretty good pitcher coming out of high school, and yet they completely altered my mechanics. It was as if they could have cared less about the pitches I was throwing to go with the mechanics.
>
> When I was traded to the Braves the one thing that gave me all the confidence in the world was Leo telling me to forget about mechanics and to put the emphasis on upgrading the quality of my pitches—to throw pitches that would get the hitters out.
>
> Young pitchers need to learn how to throw the pitches properly; I had a live enough arm that once I upgraded my pitches everything else—including mechanics—fell right into place.

We'll discuss each pitch—the grip, how to throw it, the nuances—to get you headed in the right direction.

Fastballs

You can choose from two different fastballs:

• the *four-seam* fastball, which you grip across the horseshoe (baseball lingo for the four seams on the baseball); and

• the *two-seam* fastball, which you grip *with the seams.* Your two fingers are actually resting on—touching—the seams.

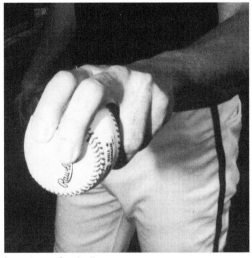

four-seam fastball

Remember the seams are put on a baseball for a specific reason. I see so many guys gripping a fastball with their fingertips resting on the slick part of the ball. You want your fingertips on the seams so you can *pull with your fingers. You pull on the ball to create backspin; if you're changing direction on the ball you will have friction—that's because your fingertips are resting on the seams of the baseball.*

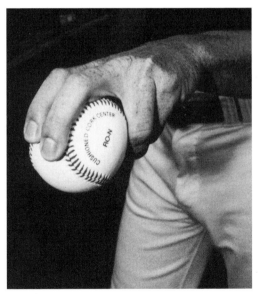

two-seam fastball sinker

four-seam fastball

two-seam fastballs

The reason why the seams are on the baseball is to get a better spin—whether it's backspin on the fastball or a curve/slider spin on a breaking ball.

The faster the ball spins, the more it moves. With a breaking ball, the faster the spin, the sharper the break. On a four-seam fastball, the faster the spin, the more power in the pitch. The faster the two-seamer spins, the more action it will have, and that means the ball will sink.

Maddux throws a two-seam fastball, and he gets it to sink on both sides of the plate.

Glavine throws a two-seam fastball, though occasionally he will go to a four-seam fastball—the power fastball.

Smoltz throws the four-seam, or power, fastball.

Neagle throws both a two-seam and a four-seam fastball.

Little League pitchers should start off with the four-seam fastball. If your hands are small it's OK to throw this pitch with three fingers, only make sure that you are still going across the horseshoe (the four seams). When your hands are big enough you can graduate to throwing the fastball with two fingers—but you'll stick with the four-seamer for now.

The beauty of this pitch is that you can feel it *pull across the seams. That pull equates to backspin. And the net result is a more accurate pitch.*

The rule of thumb is that the four-seam fastball is for power and the two-seam fastball is for movement. But there's nothing written in stone about which pitch will work better for you. Charlie Leibrandt didn't throw particularly hard, yet he preferred the four-seam fastball because it gave him better location. In a lot of cases it's just a personal matter—what feels most comfortable for your style of pitching.

A fly ball/strikeout pitcher like a John Smoltz is better suited to the power fastball. A ground ball pitcher like Greg Maddux is better suited to the two-seam fastball. But I'm not going to clone pitchers and tell every guy to follow a preconceived path.

Not every pitcher has to throw a sinking fastball, which is what you get from the two-seamer. Smoltz isn't going to throw a sinking fastball. He doesn't need to pitch that way because he can be more effective by sticking with his strengths as a power pitcher.

Denny Neagle got in trouble when he first joined the Braves because he was trying to emulate the style of Tom Glavine. I had to call Neagle over and tell him not to pitch like Glavine but stay true to his own style. He needs to pitch in quads: up and out, up and in, down and in, down and away. And he throws more breaking balls than Glavine will during the course of a game.

Don't screw around with a bunch of crazy grips. The bottom line is that you need to be able to throw the fastball for strikes and the grip has a lot to do with your ability to control the pitch.

Everything revolves around the fastball. The Braves' pitchers constantly work on commanding the fastball. A great breaking ball won't be effective unless you can work off the fastball.

Breaking Balls

There's no one set grip for throwing a breaking ball. Your grip will vary depending on your style. What we use here in Atlanta is a curveball/slider/Atlanta Braves' quality breaking ball. In other words, the way we teach it with the Braves, the curveball and slider become virtually one pitch—what we refer to as a quality breaking ball.

Grip

The ball is centered in your hand (the thumb is on the bottom, and your fingers are on the top), with either a two- or four-seam grip.

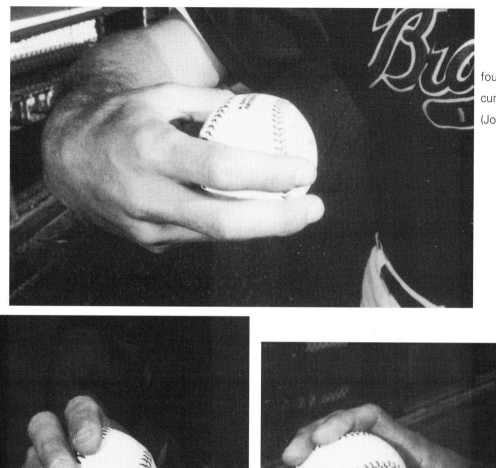

four-sear
curve ba
(John Sm

cutter/slider (Greg Maddux)

cutter/slider (Greg Maddux)

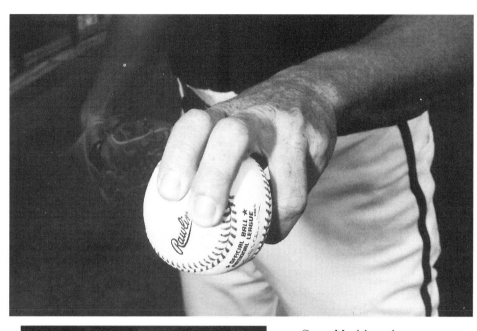

slider
(Tom
Glavine)

curve ball (Greg Maddux)

Greg Maddux throws a two-seam breaking ball. The ball is centered in his hand, but the seams are off to the side.

Tom Glavine throws a four-seam breaking ball, only the seams are off center a little bit; however, the ball is still centered in his hand.

How old should a pitcher be before he throws the breaking ball?

My answer to that frequently asked question is that it's a very individual matter; it's a function of physical coordination, and that level will vary from person to person. I've seen 13-year-old boys who can't throw a breaking ball and 11-year-old boys who have no problem with it. But if a youngster can throw one properly, then there's no reason not to let him throw the pitch.

In most cases, if you have the coordination to throw a fastball properly you can also learn to throw a breaking ball.

Three Steps to Throwing a Breaking Ball

The goal is to throw the ball first, before worrying about putting any breaking-ball spin on the pitch—we're not going to worry about spinning the ball early on in the delivery, as that gets too complex.

I teach the throw-and-turn breaking ball. At the top of the delivery your palm is facing the hitter. You want to (1) throw, (2) turn—this is where you put spin on the ball—and (3) pull the elbow in (toward your body) to protect it from overextension.

John Smoltz is a proponent of the throw-and-turn breaking ball; it's been a big help to him throughout his career with the Braves. Here's what he has to say about it:

> The whole idea behind the throw-and-turn breaking ball is to get a bigger break while cushioning the elbow. A lot of pitching coaches try to get you to spin the ball at the top of the delivery, where your hand is still behind your head (before you've thrown the pitch), and that's much harder to do. The throw-and-turn breaking ball allowed me to master more of the strike zone while getting a sharper break on the pitch.

You can find variations on this technique. The farther you extend, the smaller the break; the more you pull in, the bigger the break. When you extend farther with a smaller break, the pitch is going to be called a slider; when you pull in more—with more spin—it's going to be called a curveball.

The Difference Between Curves and Sliders

If you're looking for a smaller break (which baseball people call a slider), you throw, turn, and pull in, but you extend the arm a little farther—you don't extend it completely because that can hurt your elbow.

The goal in throwing this breaking ball is not higher velocity. It's not a *nasty curve* or a *nasty slider,* but a quality breaking ball, and we'll let the opposition call it what they want.

When we talk about throwing the breaking ball first before you turn it—well, even Greg Maddux had never heard of that idea before he joined the Braves' organization. But Johnny Sain taught it that way, and Johnny Sain was the greatest breaking-ball teacher in the history of the game; make no mistake about it.

Sain would say: *"Throw it first before you turn it and then watch it turn the corner and go down."*

My perspective is that this gives you a full turn on the ball, a better spin. The throw-turn-and-pull delivers a better breaking pitch in a more natural mechanical delivery. It's a lot easier on your arm, and you will get the results you're looking for—a great break with both fingers on the ball and both fingers spinning the ball.

Think about that. Visualize it. It makes all the sense in the world.

It doesn't matter how hard you try to throw this pitch. Don't confuse effort with spin. If you have a live spin, the pitch will break sharply; if you don't have a live spin, it won't break sharply.

I'll be working with a pitcher and tell him to throw the breaking ball slower but spin it faster, and all of a sudden—whoosh—he gets that sharp break.

Controlling the Breaking Ball

You can't learn anything about throwing the breaking ball for strikes if it's in the dirt all the time. Start throwing the breaking ball higher and see what happens. See where it goes. You have to understand how big or how small it's going to break. Pick out a spot where to start the pitch and then see where it's going to finish (after it breaks).

This will vary from pitcher to pitcher. I will tell Smoltz to start a breaking ball at the catcher's left shoulder and sweep it down and away off the plate—he'll sweep it down and away off the plate, but he'll start it in the strike zone. Therefore, his break is pretty big. Again, the size of the break determines the start and finish position of the pitch, and improving your location with the breaking ball will take practice and hard work.

Individuality—Again

If you already know how to throw a slider or a curveball and it's an effective pitch, don't change the way you throw it to adjust to the throw-pull-and-turn method that I teach. There's more than one way to throw a quality breaking ball. If it isn't broken, don't try to fix it.

But if you are struggling with your breaking ball, here's what you do: Keep the same grip you're using right now, but remember the "throw it first before you turn it" technique. This will work just fine for you.

Denny Neagle has a little slider he throws down and away and a big backdoor curve. He has his own style of grip, but he incorporates the throw and turn behind that grip and it has helped him improve the effectiveness of the breaking ball.

One last thing on the throw-and-turn method is that waiting to put the spin on the ball prevents you from creating the pitch too early. If you create the pitch too early, whether it's powering up on a fastball at the top of the delivery or starting the breaking ball too soon, I honestly believe that you take a lot away from the quality of that pitch.

The Perfect Delivery for the Throw-and-Turn Breaking Ball

At the top of the delivery your palm is facing the hitter. Start forward to throw the pitch. Then you want to change the direction of the spin and start spinning the ball, turning it in toward you and pulling it in (to make the ball spin faster) before releasing the baseball out over your front leg.

Change-up

The change-up takes on more importance as you progress to the higher levels of competition. How much you rely on the change-up depends on how fast you can throw a baseball.

No matter how hard you throw, though, you'd better remember that a good hitter can time a jet coming through that strike zone if he sees it often enough.

What the Braves' pitchers do extremely well is command their fastball away and change speeds. You will get hitters out with stuff, movement, location, change of speeds, and motion.

Hitting is a matter of timing. It's your job as a pitcher to throw off that timing. When you throw off that timing you will get that hitter out. It's simple!

Learning How to Throw the Change-up

I want you to throw a fastball, whether it's a two-seam or four-seam pitch, and put a little extra on it. Now throw a fastball and don't put the extra (velocity) on it—that's how you learn how to throw the change-up.

If you tell a young pitcher to throw a change-up, the tendency is to toss a balloon right over the heart of the plate—a nothing pitch.

The trick to throwing a change-up is finding a grip that will let you throw a fastball without as much velocity. If you can use your typical fastball grip to throw the change, then you've got it made, because this pitch is easier to command and it's deceptive.

But it requires a great deal of concentration and mental discipline to make that adjustment from a fastball with a little extra on it and a fastball without that extra velocity—which is, of course, the change-up.

The change-up is really nothing more than a batting practice fastball—same spin on the ball, same arm action—and I guarantee you no one will recognize it as a change when the pitch comes out of your hand.

Think of a change-up this way: It has the least amount of velocity you can take off your fastball and still be effective.

The goal is to maintain arm speed. Arm speed promotes deception. Deception gets the hitter out.

Location A change-up should be over the plate and down. If you throw the pitch to that location and you maintain arm speed and maximize deception, then the hitter will either swing and miss or make contact—weakly—for an out.

Grips Neagle, Smoltz, Glavine, and Maddux all throw two-seam circle changes, which is gripped with the index finger tucked against the thumb and

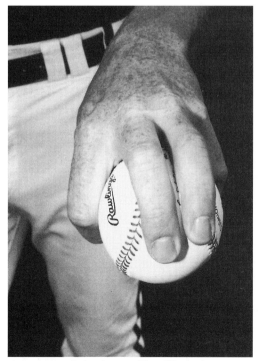
two-seam circle change (Tom Glavine)

two-seam circle change (Greg Maddux)

ring and middle fingers along the seams. The ball slides off those fingers, with the principal force directed alongside the ball, which reduces the speed of the pitch while enhancing its deception.

I will tell you one thing right now: I know for a fact that a lot of times hitters know that Maddux and Glavine are going to throw a change-up and still can't hit the pitch.

Why?

Maddux and Glavine have such great arm speed, the pitch is deceptive enough to throw off hitters' timing—even if they know it's coming!

Glavine started using his change-up more often in 1991, and it made a big difference in his career. He throws a two-seam circle change (his two middle fingers are touching the seams while thumb and index finger touch on the side of the baseball to form the circle) that's about 8 mph slower than his fastball. It comes in on the hitter just like his fastball and then—at the last instant—it sinks or (in baseball lingo) fades.

Release The goal is to release the ball naturally, just like a fastball. Accelerate at the point of release—don't back down at the last instant to take something off the pitch. Glavine and Maddux get the ball to sink because the hand has a tendency to go over the top of the baseball on the point of release—we'll call this *pronation*.

You get a little bit of pull from the two middle fingers, and this creates an over-the-top spin; the spin is from left to right for a left-handed pitcher and from right to left for a right-handed pitcher.

Now the ball is heading in on the hitter just like a two-seam fastball, only it fades on the same angle as a fastball; with the change of speeds and all that movement you are going to mess with a hitter's timing.

One other option is the four-seam circle change: two middle fingers across the four seams, thumb and index finger touching to form a circle on the side of the baseball. With the four-seamer you get a change of speeds with more backspin—the ball is rotating backward instead of over the top and you get the same look as a four-seam fastball, but it's heading in a lot slower and the hitter will be way out in front on the pitch.

The name of the game is deception, convincing the hitter that he's getting a fastball. That's why I recommend staying with the grip you selected on your fastball:

• Pitchers who throw a two-seam fastball should stick with a two-seam circle change.

• Pitchers who throw a four-seam fastball can go with either a two-seam or a four-seam circle change.

Regardless of your particular grip, always remember the golden rule: Approach your change-up as the pitch with the least amount you can take off your fastball and still be effective.

That "least amount" business will vary from one pitcher to the next.

Charlie Leibrandt threw an 80-mph fastball and it looked like it was 100 mph because his change-up was 72 mph. Maddux throws his fastball at 86 mph and his change at 79 mph; Glavine throws an 87–88-mph fastball, and his change-up is 80–81 mph.

Glavine, as I mentioned previously, has used the change as one of the cornerstones of his success. But at what point do you introduce a new pitch to your repertoire in a game situation? Glavine tells you how it's done; then we'll move along to the finer points of mechanics and delivery:

> It's like anything else—you have to spend some time practicing until you're comfortable with it so that when you do try the pitch in a game you have a fairly well-developed sense of confidence.
>
> Practice it as much as you can—whether it's pitching on the side or playing catch—until you can throw it where you want about 5 out of

every 10 pitches. Now you can try it in a game to see how successful it is.

I do not recommend that you experiment with a new pitch in a game the first time you throw it off the mound.

Two reasons:

(1) If you don't throw the pitch properly, you run the risk of getting injured.

(2) If you try it too soon and don't get the results you're looking for, you may ditch the pitch—despite the fact that it could turn out to be a good pitch down the road.

Keep throwing it on the side until you can get the location you want 8 out of 10 times. You're searching for a comfort zone, where you feel as confident throwing it in a game as you do when you're playing catch and there's no one around to pass judgment on that pitch—or to hit it a long, long way.

Chapter 3
Mechanics and Delivery

Fine-tuning your mechanics all starts with one basic question: Where should you stand on the rubber of the pitching mound? The answer to this question is not as clear-cut as you may think.

Tom Glavine stands on the third-base side of the rubber when he pitches—even though conventional wisdom teaches that left-handed pitchers stand on the first-base side and right-handed pitchers stand on the third-base side. This alignment is supposed to give you a better angle on the hitter.

So what the heck is Glavine, a lefty, doing on the third-base side? His fastball sinks and fades. His change-up fades. He wants to start on the third-base side of the rubber to catch more of the plate and to give him the proper angle to the right-handed hitter.

The lesson here is that you can't generalize about where to stand on the mound. You have to experiment to determine what's going to work best for your personal style of pitching.

When Steve Avery, another lefty hurler, pitched for the Atlanta Braves in the early nineties, he preferred to stand on the first-base side because he had a power fastball and a sharp breaking ball. Glavine has the sinker and the change, so he wants his angle on the third-base side.

Different styles. Different angles. Different starting points on the mound.

You don't try to clone pitchers; however, there are certain rules that do apply to all pitchers.

Analyzing the Pitching Motion

The windup begins with a small step back, or you can take a small step to the side. But the step must be small so that your weight doesn't shift to the back or to the side. As you take the step back, your hands begin to move. Now you have several options: You can lift your arms straight back over your head or bring them up to your face or only as high as the letters.

Tom Glavine
A Case Study of a Compact Delivery for a Left-handed Pitcher

Glavine's left foot is on the rubber and his right foot is on the dirt area on the third-base side at the start of his windup. He takes a small step back with his right foot, and his arms come to letter height—not over his head. He plants his left foot in front of the rubber to drive and brings his right leg up with a more pronounced hip turn than Maddux; Glavine's right leg and hip, therefore, are a little past the point where they are square with the rubber.

He breaks his hands out of the glove at the letters—left hand over the ball, getting it cocked to unload the pitch—and starts his weight shift forward with some flex in his landing leg. Glavine gets to his high three-quarter or overhand slot and releases the ball out over his front leg—the right. The back leg—the left—comes around for his follow-through toward home plate to finish the pitch.

Greg Maddux
A Case Study of a Compact Delivery for a Right-handed Pitcher

Maddux has both feet on the rubber and takes a small step back with the left foot and brings his arms over his head to start his windup. He turns on his right foot and plants it in front of the rubber to drive with; he lifts his left leg up with a hip turn until his left leg and hip are square with the rubber.

The left leg comes back down and his right hand comes out of the glove—the hand is over the ball with the grip of whatever pitch he is throwing—and his arm comes out and up to his high three-quarter or overhand unloading position, which is also referred to as his arm slot. He starts forward with his stride; the landing leg is flexed or bent.

The pitch is released out over the front leg (his left), and after the pitch is released his back leg (his right) comes around and follows through to bring his body forward and finish the pitch. His weight shifts toward the target—home plate—and he is careful not to raise his head up too high, as this will shift his weight away from home plate.

Despite their differences, both Glavine and Maddux unload the pitch from a high three-quarter to overhand unloading position. And each pitcher uses the same timing mechanism for delivering the pitch—one, two, three, four, boom. This is what I call cadence, a means to either speed up or slow down a delivery.

The cadence is a rhythm or timing device that prevents you from moving too slow or too fast. A delivery has to be coordinated and precise so that everything comes together when you release the ball.

Cadence

On the count of *one* you take a small step back and bring your arms over your head or to the letters.

On the count of *two* you plant your foot in front of the rubber and lift your lead leg—the leg kick—to be squared up with the rubber.

On the count of *three* you shift your weight forward, break your hands, and bring the pitching arm into its unloading position—the high three-quarter or overhand slot.

On the count of *four* you release the pitch.

Mechanical Flaws

Check out these typical mechanical woes:

- a fast bottom half (lower body) and a slow upper half (upper body),
- your front leg starting to race,
- dragging your hands, and
- collapsing the back side of your body on the delivery.

This last item requires some explanation. Tom Seaver perfected a delivery known as *drop and drive*—you push off the rubber and drop down to release the pitch. In the real world very few pitchers can get away with this delivery.

What we've discovered with the Braves is that if you stand tall on the back side, the downhill angle to the hitter is much better. Sure, you want to drive and bend a little bit, but many pitchers collapse the back side too much and before they know it one of the coaches is yelling, "Hey, buddy; you're underneath the ball!"

What the heck does that mean?

Your back side is going down, your front side is going up, and now you're pitching on a tilt and your pitches are going to be off target.

When it comes to mechanics I'll give you a little bit of advice—less motion is always better. With more motion in your delivery you increase the chances for something to go wrong.

Maddux and Glavine have very simple mechanics. A cadence of one, two, three, four, boom—deliver the pitch. They don't start off slow and then move fast; they don't start off fast and all of a sudden try to slow it all down. They have the same cadence, or rhythm, all the way through. There's no wasted motion. It's an uncomplicated, easy delivery.

Checkpoints A checkpoint is something a pitcher must repeat every time he pitches to keep every aspect of the delivery in harmony. Or, in some cases, a checkpoint can be a troubleshooting mechanism to prevent a pitcher from getting into bad habits. Maddux has three checkpoints, and believe me, any pitcher can benefit from learning from Maddux's checkpoints. It's pretty hard to argue with his success:

(1) Wherever Maddux's head goes, the body must follow. He can't tilt his

head from side to side. He can't raise his head too high. He can't tilt his head back.

(2) He wants to break his hands from the glove to get to an imaginary box that encircles his unloading position—baseball lingo: the arm slot. He imagines his hand coming through that box the same way every single time—regardless of the particular pitch.

(3) He wants to step in the direction of the pitch. If he's pitching the ball to the

outer half of the plate, he wants to step toward the outer half; if he's pitching the ball to the inner half, he wants to step toward the inner half; if he's going down the middle, he wants to step down the middle.

Glavine's checkpoints are as follows:
(1) He wants to break his hands quickly from the glove to get him to his high three-quarter position to unload the pitch.
(2) Same as Maddux's third checkpoint.

Smoltz has one checkpoint:
(1) When he comes out of the glove he doesn't want to drop his hands too low because that puts some punishment on his arm.

And here are Neagle's checkpoints:
(1) He wants to make sure he does not pitch from side to side. In other words, he wants to go forward and down instead of pulling out to the side—shifting toward third base instead of toward home plate.
(2) He has to avoid trying to muscle the ball on the back side. He's learning how to be more relaxed. In the past he had a tendency to create the pitch too early.

Heck, learning proper mechanics should not be as taxing as taking a geometry quiz. I want the learning curve on this chapter to be quick and painless.

I like to compare throwing a baseball to driving an automobile. If you drive a car and the steering wheel has too much play in it, what are you going to do? You're forced to move your arms around all over the place to get going in the right direction.

A pitching delivery works pretty much the same way. If you have too much play in a delivery, you're forced to overcompensate through movement; it's a less precise way to throw the pitch in the intended direction.

The last thing you need in a delivery is to be flipping and flopping like a fish out of water. Keep the delivery compact. Firm everything up. Excess motion should be avoided.

The Basic Posture for a Delivery

If you get confused by anything you've read in this chapter, you can always refer back to the cardinal rule of pitching posture—get yourself into position to throw a punch as you deliver the baseball.

Pitchers at all levels have a pretty good idea of how to throw a punch. It's an easy stance to visualize. That's why I use this analogy to remind pitchers—even Tom Glavine—to throw the baseball, instead of slinging it, toward home plate. If you sling a baseball, you are overextended, flopping around and moving forward before you are ready to unload the pitch. The throw-the-punch position is just another way of emphasizing the need for a compact delivery.

Individuality and Pitching Mechanics

OK, I've told you many times that I don't believe in cloning pitchers, and I'll provide you with one more example. You will see right-handed pitchers after releasing the pitch falling off to the first-base side and left-handed pitchers falling off to the third-base side. I don't see anything wrong with that—as long as it's momentum that is carrying the pitcher off the mound in that direction.

If you throw the ball to home plate and you have generated so much power that momentum has caused you to fall off to the first-base side (if you're a righty) or third-base side (if you're a lefty), that's all good.

What you don't want to do, though, is throw the baseball while you are falling off to either the first-base or the third-base side. Now you are pulling off the ball and you're losing the power—and the effectiveness—of the pitch.

Something I have problems with—and pitchers at all levels tend to do this—is trying to stop the natural forces of momentum so that you are ready to field your position. If you try to stop yourself in a delivery you increase the risk of an arm injury.

I want to see a natural flow all the way through the delivery because it takes pressure off your arm as you deliver the baseball.

I don't care about the bunt or the ground ball back up the middle. If a hitter wants to bunt on me because I'm falling off to one side or the other, but my stuff is awesome, then I'll take my chances.

We'll get into this subject once again when the topic turns to fielding, but the bottom line is that you don't compromise your stuff and risk an injury to field a bunt or a grounder. You have other infielders to help you out on this play, and more often than not your reactions will take over when a ball is hit up the middle of the diamond.

Public Enemy Number One Never try to make the pitch do more than you can physically make it do. You will overexert, screw up the effectiveness of the pitch, and risk hurting your arm—a very precious commodity. You can only give 100 percent effort on any skill or task. There's no such thing as putting out 110 percent effort on a pitch.

All I'm asking you to do is give 100 percent to make your mechanics smooth, compact, and under control. Follow the examples of Maddux, Glavine, Smoltz, and Neagle and you cannot go wrong.

Chapter 4
Strategies and Tactics

Many of the pitching gurus through the years have tried to overcomplicate the art of pitching. I like to keep it simple. In working with the Braves, I tell my pitchers to focus on being in command of the fastball, learn how to throw the down-and-away strike consistently, and change speeds to keep the hitters off balance. That is the primary strategy, regardless of whether it's opening day or the seventh game of the World Series.

If a pitcher doesn't have command of the fastball, he has nothing. Tom Glavine has been able to get by with a great change of speeds. But the only times he struggles is when the fastball is off target.

Let me give you an example of how important the fastball is to all pitchers. Terrell Wade, our number five starting pitcher in 1997 before he was selected by the Tampa Bay Devil Rays in the expansion draft, was struggling early in a game against the Montreal Expos. Wade, a power pitcher at the time, was trying to spot the ball and in so doing was sacrificing stuff to hit location. When you throw to spots there's a tendency to float the pitch into the hitter's wheelhouse; the next thing you know the ball is rocketing into the gaps or out of the park.

That's what happened to T. Wade. Six of the first eight Expo hitters connected with solid line drives. Then, when he began to work off his fastball and stopped nibbling around the plate to hit spots, he was much more successful. He was going with his strengths and being aggressive. You have to pitch aggressively if you expect to gain the upper hand.

Of course you will have a strategy each time you face a hitter, but the specific strategy will vary from one pitcher to the next. Greg Maddux, Tom Glavine, John Smoltz, and Denny Neagle are all going to pitch somewhat differently to the same hitter. I'll say it again: I don't believe in cloning pitchers.

But before we get into the unique situations and styles of pitching, the nuances of the craft, remember the basic strategy for a pitcher: command of the fastball, especially the down-and-away strike, and a change of speeds. If you can do those two things—and I don't care if you're a major league pitcher or a topflight college pitcher or a kid in high school or Little League—then you will be successful at any level.

A lot of times in high school a young pitcher can power his way through—he's trying to strike out a lot of guys and impress the scouts. That's fine for high school, but once you face competition as good as you are you're going to struggle.

The solution is combining a command of the fastball with a change of speeds. You do those things and you will have success.

I know some of you are thinking that I'm oversimplifying this process. My job is to simplify and demystify the art of pitching. It's worked for the Braves' staff and it will work for you.

You don't have to take my word for it; here's John Smoltz with some good advice:

> We tend to complicate the game of baseball more than is necessary. When you're out there pitching, the objective is to keep things as simple as possible. That's the best policy. When you get into slumps you tend to make changes. Hitters do it. Pitchers do it. The concept is that

there has to be something wrong instead of going back to the basic principles of pitching. That's what Leo's system of instruction is all about. The old-time drills; simple, pragmatic advice; the things you need to snap you out of that funk that's getting in the way of success.

Pitching with Men on Base

Pitchers often try to power their way through a men-on-base jam, using supercontrol or superstuff to stop a potential big inning. All this approach will do is make matters worse.

When you try to put too much emphasis on control, your control actually gets worse, the pitches are off target, and you don't give yourself any room to work. If you try to get out of a bind with superstuff, that means you're probably overthrowing. What happens when you overthrow? You go off target; you start missing.

So you have to be strong enough mentally to know that you can't go overboard with trying to be too fine with your control or trying consciously to blow guys away with great stuff.

It's not all that bad if one run scores in an inning. You can have one run score in an inning four times during a game and if you're a starter you still have a chance to go nine innings. If you have a three-run inning, though, you're not going nine and if you're in the National League you'll probably be pinch-hit for in the fifth or sixth inning.

The name of the game is damage control. Ideally, you'd like to get out of the inning with no runs crossing the plate, but you have to remain firm in your conviction that you must continue to pitch as if there's no one on base . . . even if the bases are loaded.

If it's a close game you've got to be careful. And there's always the added distraction of a fast runner on base. But you can't throw a pitch when you're dividing your attention equally between the runner and the hitter; you never want to get caught in between. The priority is always the hitter.

Pitchers struggle with men on base at every level, from Little League to the big leagues. I give everyone the same advice—remain firm and throw the pitch with conviction.

Say that you're pitching with the bases loaded and you walk the hitter and a run scores. Chances are there will be someone getting all worked up over the fact that you walked in a run. But what we believe here in Atlanta is that it's not always that bad to walk the hitter in this situation, especially when you fall behind in the count.

The underlying principle is that you do not want to give in to the strike zone. I'm not talking about giving in to the hitter. I don't care who is at the plate or what team he's playing for. You want to stay stubborn on the edge. So when you're pitching with the bases loaded or with runners on second and third, why give in to the strike zone and bring the ball back over the heart of the plate?

I'll let Tom Glavine give you a specific example of what I'm talking about:

I was pitching against the Cardinals and Ron Gant was up there with a 3–2 count. I was torn about what to do in this spot, but I decided not to walk him, so I threw a fastball in for a strike and—bam—he hit a home run.

This was a solo shot, so it didn't hurt that much, but you always have reminders—no matter how good you are—that you just can't throw a strike right over the middle. If you're caught in-between on a pitch and you're not sure if it's the right thing to do, nine times out of ten something bad will happen.

That pitch to Gant was an example of the wrong strategy; now here's an example of the right strategy. I'm pitching against the Cincinnati Reds a couple of years ago. It's the first inning and I'm in a mess of trouble. One run is in, the bases are loaded with one out, and I'm facing Kevin Mitchell, a good right-handed power hitter.

The temptation, of course, is to throw him a strike so that I don't walk in the run. But I don't give in to the strike zone; instead, I walk Mitchell and a second run comes across. I get the next hitter to ground into an inning-ending double play; I retire the next 18 batters in order; and we go on to win the game, 5–2.

I could have given Mitchell a good pitch to hit because I didn't want to walk him and then I'm down 5–0 and out of the ball game. As it turned out, I probably won that game in the first inning. There's a big difference between being down 2–0 and 5–0 in the first inning.

The strategy is "don't give in to the strike zone." It's the one thing you must remember if you want to become a successful pitcher. It's not a matter of giving in to a hitter. The mentality is not to even care about the hitter per se—it's the strike zone that you want to focus on.

Bouncing Back from Failure

Dealing with failure is one of the toughest things a pitcher has to learn. As a coach, I know I can push my pitchers harder when things are going well. If we're on a roll right now and the guys are pitching well, that's when I can get on them to make certain improvements. Even Glavine and Maddux can always get better; every pitcher can afford to improve on some aspect of his game.

Maddux has this to say:

> Failure is the best teacher in the world; you get to learn from what happens to you—both good and bad—in a real-live game situation. I've given up a lot of runs in my career, and that means I've made a lot of mistakes and I've had a chance to learn from them. It's usually easy to figure out what you're doing wrong. The hitters have a funny way of telling you that a particular pitch isn't working.
>
> I'm well aware of what's going on behind me when I pitch a game. If a batter hits a pea rod to left off the wall for a double. If the infielders are diving all over the place, sort of a highlight film from one batter to the next, then I know I'd better make some adjustments; heck, if you give up a bunch of runs you can't get rattled and let it affect your performance the rest of the game. You have to make improvements.
>
> Evaluate your performance after each game you pitch—whether you had a terrible outing or you hurled a perfect game. Stop and think about the things you did right and the things you need to change before you come back out there and do it all over again.

The wrong time to push is when a pitcher has had a tough game or a string of bad outings. Paul Byrd, a reliever whom we picked up from the Mets in the Greg McMichael trade, gave up a grand slam one night at Turner Field.

The next day, when we were on the side getting our throwing in, I went over to him and we discussed what went wrong with that pitch; I was certainly not going to make an issue of it right after he gave up a home run.

Young pitchers have a tendency to second-guess themselves after making a mistake. It's usually not so much a question of what pitch was thrown but the location it was thrown to.

Look at what happened to Mark Wohlers at the 1996 World Series when Jim Leyritz hit the home run against him. All you heard after the game was: "How could Wohlers throw Leyritz a slider instead of a 100-mph fastball? Was he crazy?"

No, he wasn't crazy.

If Mark had gotten the slider down and away, Leyritz would not have had a chance to hit that pitch. And if Wohlers threw a fastball and Leyritz hit it for a home run, then you'd hear that Wohlers was throwing too many fastballs and the Yankees were just sitting back and waiting on that one pitch.

Here's what Wohlers has to say about the 1996 World Series:

> One thing you learn from experience is that you determine what pitch you're going to throw, you believe in the pitch, and you throw it. There's no second-guessing. Sure, you can look back and feel like there was something you could have done differently.
>
> But to be honest, I still feel like I threw the right pitch to Leyritz; it was simply in the wrong location. I've gotten beat on my second-best pitch, but at times you need to fail to get better; you have to learn from your mistakes.

My best pitch is the fastball. But what am I going to do—throw nothing but fastballs? I tried that and got sent down to the minor leagues three times. I never second-guess myself. If the location to Leyritz had been where I wanted it, then the outcome would have been quite different.

It all comes down to location, not pitch selection. It's not just that you have to throw the right pitch; it's more that it has to go to the intended part of the plate. That's why it's ridiculous to make a federal case over what pitch to throw in a given situation; where you throw the pitch will have much more to do with your success or failure.

But let's say that you do fail to get the job done. Put it behind you right away. I tell my pitchers that I don't want anything negative to carry over from one pitch to the next.

That's what Maddux does:

Whether you just threw a great pitch or the worst pitch in history, the only thing that really matters is your next pitch. You are only as good as your next pitch, right?

Another specific example from the Atlanta Braves' archives: We're in Florida playing the Marlins and Mike Bielecki is protecting a one-run lead and there's two outs and two runners on base. Bielecki thinks that the hitter committed to the pitch—check swing and the ball game is over. The umpire says he didn't swing. It's ball four and so now Bielecki is all unglued. I go out to the mound to talk to him, and he's trying to tell me that the hitter went around.

Forget about that last hitter—that guy is long gone and he's standing on first base. I told Bielecki to put all his attention on the next hitter because one more out and we win the game. He has two choices with this hitter: He can tighten up, rear back, muscle up, and go for superpower. Or he can be loose and live and attack the way he knows how, just going with his natural delivery and his best stuff.

He takes option number two, strikes out the next hitter on three pitches, and we win the game.

The moral of this story is that you can't allow your last pitch to interfere with the quality of your next pitch; the rule is no carryover from one pitch to the next.

The same rule applies to letting one bad start affect the next start. Smoltz has learned this lesson from experience:

> I had a great year in 1997, though on paper it didn't look quite as impressive as my Cy Young season in 1996. I had only one bad start the entire year (1997), and, unfortunately, it happened against the team that originally signed me—the Detroit Tigers. I got caught up in all the hype surrounding that game, all the memories of growing up in Michigan and playing in the Tigers' minor league system. I changed my routine, went out, and pitched a terrible game—I didn't make good pitches—and lost. It was one of those games you're going to have, but I wished it hadn't happened against the team I grew up playing for. But I rebounded quickly with two solid starts—that ability to fight back is what it takes to pitch in the big leagues and to be successful at any level of competition.
>
> Greg Maddux gave me a great tip once: When things are going great you'd better remember how you're doing it because you're going to need that information when the hard times come around.
>
> This is so true. When I won 14 games in a row it happened so quickly; I tried to remember what I was doing right because I knew that it would come in handy when I got into trouble down the road.

If you give up a solo home run it's no big deal. Don't lose your focus on throwing strikes. You can give up four solo shots in a ball game and still go nine innings.

Kent Mercker gave up three solo shots against Cincinnati in 1995. He pitched a four-hitter and lost 3–1 but went eight innings. But one three-run homer and you're probably not going to get a chance to go the distance.

Mercker, of course, pitched a brilliant no-hitter for the Braves on April 8, 1994, at Dodger Stadium. It was early in the season, and he came over to me in the dugout after the seventh inning to say he was getting tired. I told him to look up at the scoreboard and check out what was happening. He knew he was pitching a no-hitter but had lost track of the innings and thought—mistakenly—that it was only the sixth inning. Once he realized it was already after the seventh, he relaxed and went on to finish the job.

Mercker threw 133 pitches that night, but when you have an opportunity to pitch a no-hitter you should shove the pitch count aside and go for it—as long as there's nothing physically wrong with your arm. It's a once-in-a-lifetime chance.

I know that some people would say that you run the risk of hurting the pitcher; go tell that to the guy who is throwing the no-hitter and see what he has to say about it!

Whitey Ford always told me to shoot for nine innings and 125 pitches. In a game in 1997 I had John Smoltz throw 128 pitches, including 103 fastballs—and every one of those pitches was on the outside part of the plate. Smoltz was consistent with the down-and-away fastball the entire game, and the Los Angeles Dodgers didn't have a chance against him.

That's what I mean when I talk about the necessity of commanding the fastball and being consistent with the down-and-away strike. Once you put that strategy into play it will make a huge difference.

The goal for all pitchers is to throw twice as many strikes as balls over the course of a game. If the ratio slips to 60–40 or 50–50, then you are no longer in command of the fastball and you're going to struggle.

You don't have to be a Curt Schilling to use the fastball as your key pitch, the one that sets everything else up in your arsenal. Charlie Leibrandt didn't throw his fastball more than 80 mph, but he won about 15 games a year for the Braves in 1991 and '92 because he had excellent command of the fastball.

It doesn't matter how hard you throw: Greg Maddux throws 85–86 mph; Tom Glavine throws 87 mph—everything works off the command—not the velocity—of the fastball.

As long as you can learn how to control your fastball and mix it in with some combination of the change-up, curveball, and slider, then you can pitch at any level.

What's wrong with baseball today? A lot of good, young pitchers get over-looked because they don't produce gaudy numbers on the stupid radar gun. Radar guns should be thrown in the garbage, where they belong. I don't care what a radar gun says; I want to see an action pitch and a hitter's reaction to a pitch.

The mentality of a pitcher has a lot to do with whether that number on the gun is meaningless or significant. I believe that it raises the risk of an arm injury if a pitcher looks up at the scoreboard and says, "Oh, my God, I'm only throwing 82 mph; I'm going to try to get it up to 90 mph."

This principle applies to pitchers at every level of competition. I tell all pitchers the same thing: Don't worry about the radar gun, because what it's telling you is meaningless. But if you tell a pitcher that he's not throwing hard enough because of the radar gun, the first thing he'll resort to is overexertion. And what causes arm injuries? Overexertion.

It's no wonder that so many pitchers hurt their arms, with all this misplaced empashis on velocity.

Pitching Ahead or Behind in the Count

Before every series I meet with the pitching staff and we analyze the strengths and weaknesses of the opposing team's hitters. This applies to every series we play, including the World Series matchups with the Cleveland Indians (1995) and New York Yankees (1996).

Now, quite obviously at the major league level we have tons of scouting reports on the other teams. But I start every meeting pretty much the same way: I tell our pitchers to get the first pitch over for a strike; if they don't, you can throw those scouting reports out the window. Everything in the report is based on working ahead in the count.

Here are some numbers to think about. In 1995, Greg Maddux gave up only 43 hits out of the 600 times he threw a first-pitch strike to the hitter. Mark Wohlers gave up only 8 or 9 hits out of the 125 times he threw a first-pitch strike. That's how rare it is for these guys to give up a hit when they get that first pitch over for a strike.

Every scouting report I read indicates that all hitters like to get a fastball on the first pitch. Frankly, I don't care if a hitter is looking for a first-pitch fastball; we're going to give it to him, and I'll tell you why. Experience has proven that if you can throw the fastball for a strike, down and away, you'll probably either get ahead in the count or record an out to start the inning. Here again we see the command-of-the-fastball, down-and-away-strike strategy in action.

Major league hitters—and I honestly believe that this carries over to Little League, high school, and college—thrive on 1–0 and 2–0 counts. On the 1–1 count you're living on the edge; it's the pitch that will determine whether you're going to pitch ahead or behind in the count. The goal is to throw strikes and get ahead in the count. It's that simple.

Tom Glavine, I'm happy to say, agrees with me:

> If I'm ahead in the count, regardless of whether it's 1–2, 0–2, or 0–1, I've got far more options in terms of what pitch I want to throw and what location I want to use, as opposed to being behind in the count; when you fall behind, the hitter is more narrowed into looking for a fastball because that's what pitchers throw most consistently for strikes.

If I'm behind in the count and a hitter is looking for a fastball, then the middle, inside part of the plate becomes a danger zone; there's not enough room in there for me to make a mistake without getting hurt. So when I'm behind in the count I'm generally going to throw a fastball or a change-up away from the hitter. If I'm ahead, it could be a fastball or change-up away; it could be a breaking ball out of the strike zone. When I'm ahead it opens up the whole plate to all my pitches and I can be a little more aggressive.

Greg Maddux puts this be-more-aggressive-as-you-get-ahead-in-the-count mentality into perspective:

The hitter is most vulnerable when you get him in an 0–2 bind. My goal is to take him out immediately. I'm going right after him, no fooling around with wasting a pitch up high or throwing one in the dirt.

Why waste a pitch on 0–2? That's the most ridiculous thing I've ever seen in the game. People are scared to death of giving up a hit on 0–2. I don't understand that at all. What do most hitters bat in 0–2 counts? It's the lowest batting average of any count. So when's the best time to get the hitter to swing at a pitch? You guessed it—0–2.

So let's say you follow conventional wisdom and you waste a pitch up high or you throw a curveball and you try to get him to swing at a pitch in the dirt. Heck, it's usually such a bad pitch that the hitter will lay off. Now you just wasted a pitch and you're also wasting time. This strategy does not help you at all. It does nothing to help you with your next pitch. If anything, it gives the hitter more of an advantage because he gets to see one more pitch come out of your hand.

You learn this waste-the-0–2 pitch stuff early on in your career. Some teams will fine a young pitcher if he gives up an 0–2 hit; they plant it in your head right away that no matter what happens you can't give up a hit on an 0–2 count. That's why batters get hit with pitches on 0–2. You also see more wild pitches and passed balls on 0–2 than on any other count.

Go after the hitter on 0–2! The guy is on the defensive; you've got him on the ropes. There are fewer homers and doubles hit on 0–2 than on any other count. Getting ahead in the count takes away a lot of power, just as falling behind 2–1 or 3–1 increases power.

This is the mentality that sets Maddux apart from the rest of us. But there's something to be learned from his example. Little League, high school, and college pitchers who get ahead 0–2 should take advantage of the hitter. When I was pitching in Catholic high school, an 0–2 count meant that it was time to go for the strikeout. I didn't want to throw the ball in the dirt or up high to waste a pitch; I was going in for the kill. To me, this is just plain old common sense.

The goal is to get ahead 0–1. But that does not mean that you should just throw the ball right over the plate. The get-me-over pitch is going to be blasted, whether it's a fastball or a breaking ball. Throw the pitch in a firm fashion, preferably down and away.

If you're going to throw the ball down the middle—generally speaking not what I'd recommend to young pitchers—make sure there's some movement on the pitch.

So if you get a strike on a down-and-away fastball, the count is 0–1, and now you have options. You can pitch inside. You can change speeds. You can get the hitter to chase a ball in the dirt.

If you don't get that first strike and you're pitching behind in the count, unless you have a super fastball or a great change-up like Tom Glavine, then it's much harder to pitch with success.

When you're behind in the count 2–1 or 3–1, you don't want to sacrifice stuff for location. I hammer on this point all the time with young pitchers. Be firm and throw a good fastball, change-up, or breaking ball. Never throw a get-me-over pitch in those counts because you'll get ripped to shreds.

If the count is 3–2 and the hitter is sitting on the fastball—hey, that's fine; let him look for it. If you can throw the 3–2 fastball for a down-and-away strike you'll get him out. But if you throw a 3–2 fastball down the middle, or a 3–2 fastball and you're trying to go inside and you don't get it in, or a 3–2 fastball and it's up and you don't get it down, then you're in trouble.

So if we're going to throw fastballs behind in the count, we're going to throw down-and-away stikes. One other advantage of mastering the down-and-away strike is that it will allow you to jam people, to pitch inside more.

Despite what you may have heard, it's harder to jam hitters if you're a right-handed pitcher throwing to a right-handed hitter or a left-handed pitcher throwing to a left-handed hitter.

Why?

You're coming from the same side of the plate, and some hitters have a tendency to give just a little bit of ground. If the hitter moves off the plate and you miss with an inside strike, then the next thing you know, he'll unload on that pitch for a double or a home run.

But if you're a right-hander throwing to a left-handed hitter or a southpaw throwing to a right-handed hitter, the angle of the pitch will allow you to get in on the batter; you can lock him up inside and jam him with the pitch—but you can only do this if you've established that you can throw that down-and-away strike.

Why does Greg Maddux pitch inside more than any other pitcher in baseball? It's simple—he's always ahead in the count. And rule number one is that you only pitch inside when you're ahead in the count.

I've heard some pitching coaches say that being able to pitch inside sets everything else up. That strategy is the exact opposite of what I teach. My pitchers with the Braves—Glavine, Maddux, Smoltz, and Neagle—use the down-and-away strike to set everything up for being able to pitch inside. I want you to do the same.

Tom Glavine knows a thing or two about pitching to both sides of the plate, against both righties and lefties:

Regardless of whether it's a right-handed hitter or a left-handed hitter, I'm going to focus on the outside part of the plate and keep the guy honest on the inner half. It's easier for a southpaw to pitch inside to a right-handed hitter; I generally will not use the inner half of the plate as much against a lefty.

But I'm still going to rely on the same pitches—fastball, slider, change-up—as I do against righties.

In the old days it was commonplace for left-handed pitchers to dominate left-handed hitters. This skill is becoming a lost art in the game today—and I see this at every level, from Little League on up through college. I know why this is happening, and there is a way to combat this trend.

It's a fact that as soon as a left-handed pitcher takes the mound, left-handed hitters automatically become high-ball hitters. If you watch the replays of games on TV you will see that left-handed hitters are teeing off on pitches that are up in the strike zone; you neutralize this by throwing the down-and-away strike. When throwing inside, you make sure that it's off the plate—don't get that pitch over the heart of the plate by mistake.

The same plan applies to right-handed pitchers throwing to right-handed hitters: Keep the ball down and away. When you throw inside it's got to be off the plate. If a hitter starts leaning over the plate to go out and get the outside pitch, you blow the ball by him. Making adjustments is part of being a complete pitcher.

It used to be said that a left-handed pitcher should never throw a change-up to a left-handed hitter, that breaking balls were the only way to go. What nonsense! Our left-handed pitchers throw change-ups down and away to left-handed hitters and we get them to roll over on the ball for a nice, easy grounder to second base. Are you going to tell Tom Glavine not to throw a change-up to a left-handed hitter? You'd have to be out of your mind. As Glavine says:

It's always been a no-no for a lefty pitcher to throw the change-up to a lefty hitter. But I was having a lot of trouble against the tough left-handed hitters like Tony Gwynn and Barry Bonds. I experimented with throwing the change-up against them and I realized that it could be just as effective against a lefty as it is against a righty.

When you face a great hitter, whether it's in Little League, high school, or college, the situation dictates how you pitch to him. You don't want to say: *Oh, here's Tony Gwynn; I can't get this guy out to save my life.*

The way you get a guy like that out is by going after him and being aggressive. But that doesn't mean you throw a strike right over the heart of the plate—do that and he'll kill you. You've got to make it a quality strike, and you have to be aggressive to the point where you don't give in to the strike zone.

I'm a fastball, sinker, change-up type of pitcher. If I'm facing a hitter and he likes the ball down and away, well, that's not going to change my plan of action—to go for the down-and-away strike. I don't care what he likes or doesn't like. I'm going to pitch *my* game, regardless of his strengths and weaknesses.

I have my pitchers follow a very simple strategy: down-and-away strikes, inside balls. It has helped make Maddux, Glavine, Smoltz, Neagle, and the rest of our guys better pitchers, and there's no reason why it won't work for you.

Chapter 5
Fielding the Position

One of the things you hear from many coaches is that once a pitcher has let the ball go, he immediately has to be in the ideal position to field a ground ball hit back up the middle or handle a bunt.

Believe it or not, one of the easiest ways to injure your arm is to stop yourself in the middle of a delivery; that's why I don't believe in telling kids to stop and square up at the end of releasing a pitch.

Fielding the position is based on a quick reaction, athleticism, and instinct, but there are certain drills you can perform to complement those God-given qualities.

Pitcher's Fielding Practice (PFP) is a series of drills that give you the rudiments of what you need to help yourself—and your team—with the glove. To explain how this works, here's Denny Neagle with an overview:

> I think of PFP as another reinforcement system for my skills—it's the same basic principle as the throwing program. The more you rehearse a mechanical process, the better equipped you'll be out on the mound in a real-live game situation.
>
> The Atlanta Braves' coaches handle PFP with the same intelligent,

pragmatic approach as with the throwing program—you do it enough to learn how it's done without reaching the point where the whole thing becomes redundant. Some teams believe you have to do 45 minutes of drills to get it right. That's not necessary.

Let's be realistic: If a ball is hit back to you under the pressure of an actual game situation, you're either going to be able to field it and make the play or not. It's a spur-of-the-moment type of deal.

It's true, though, that rehearsing the basic drills for 15 minutes will sharpen the skills you'll need to tap into in a game. That's what we do with the Braves.

All the pitchers line up and we go through these basic drills:

(1) *The comebacker:* The ball is hit right at you. Field the ball cleanly and throw it over to first. Get back in line and repeat.

(2) *Fielding the bunt:* Field the bunt—either in front of home or down the first or third-base line—cleanly and throw to first. Repeat.

(3) *A bunt hit down the third-base line for the play at second base:* Field the bunt, turn around, and throw to second base to start the double play.

(4) *Suicide or safety squeeze:* Field the ball and throw it to the catcher at home.

(5) *The comebacker, Part II:* Throw the ball home; the catcher then throws it on to first base.

(6) *Covering first base:* This general-ly applies to bunts or grounders hit to the first-base side of the infield.

Those are the six basic PFP drills you're going to practice to prepare for a game. The way we handle it here is perfect; we don't spend 45–60 minutes working on this stuff. The objective is to get the muscle memory down pat. Make the plays. Know you can do it. And you are done with it.

Fielding is what I'd call one of those supporting skills that help to make you a winning pitcher. There's more to winning ball games than just pitching well. You've got to be able to hold runners on, lay down the sacrifice bunt to move the runner into scoring position—those little things that make a big difference.

One other skill that pitchers have to work on is backing up the bases. Your coach will practice this with you—or he should—and it's something that the Braves' pitchers rehearse during spring training and in infield practice. We practice picking a runner off of second, covering third when the third baseman comes in to field the bunt, backing up the bases on outfield throws.

You don't need to spend a lot of time on this stuff, but it does have to get repeated enough so that you know what to do—and how to react—in a game; it's part of a pitcher's bag of tricks.

Greg Maddux is a great fielder; it's a pleasure to watch him in action with a glove, and this has reinforced what I already believed—that fielding the position is one more thing you can do to make your life easier.

All of our pitchers are good fielders. Greg Maddux, of course, is tremendous. Tom Glavine is awesome. Smoltz is a great fielder; Neagle is awesome, too. They all know what to do in every situation—the ball hit back up the box, being in the right place to back up the bases, and covering first base.

As Denny said, the time to go over all of this at the major league level is during spring training. We split up the pitching staff into two groups, and the group not throwing that day will do PFP.

Let me elaborate on some of the PFP drills. A lot of instructors will tell you when *covering first base* hit the inside part of the bag with your foot so you don't get spiked on a close play, and you have to hit the bag with a certain foot to ensure a proper angle.

This is what I tell my pitchers: "Get your butt over there to cover the base!" I don't care which foot you hit the bag with. I do, however, stress the importance of touching the inside part of the bag to avoid getting spiked; once again, the goal is to stay healthy so you can go to the post when it's your turn to pitch.

But I don't talk about foot angles when you're hitting the bag. All I want you to do is field the ball cleanly and get over to the bag in time to make the play. Don't try to overcomplicate this whole process or you're more likely to screw it up.

One other variable is the defensive capability of your first baseman. Some guys will feed you the ball on target, while other guys just can't seem to make this simple throw. This is why it's so important to practice this drill with your first baseman so you know what to expect when it happens in a game.

Yeah, I know it gets old in a hurry. But this drill is a good way to get some exercise and master a very important fielding technique.

The pitcher covering first on a double play: If you're a lefty, you want your left foot to touch the inside part of the bag; if you're a righty, you want your right foot to touch the inside part of the bag—this positioning helps you stretch while increasing your ability to move laterally.

On ground balls hit back to the mound during PFP, I think it's ridiculous to hit rockets at the pitcher. I hit grounders back to the pitcher so that he can field the ball cleanly and throw it to first base. It's a crime to get a pitcher injured during a fielding drill—there's no excuse for that.

On ground balls hit back to the pitcher and a throw to second base
you want to use common sense in how hard you hit the grounders. Teaching
fundamentals is designed to demonstrate how a particular skill is mastered, not
to show a guy how to screw things up by presenting a worst-case scenario.

Charging bunts and all the bunt plays to all the bases are extremely
important, and I'll tell you why: When a hitter lays down a bunt he is doing you
a favor; he is giving you an out, so take it—don't give it away.

If it's going to be a close play at second and an easy play at first, I'd rather you
take the easy out. Always go for the sure out. There're three outs in an inning,
and then you only need to get two.

Backing up the bases: Don't make a big deal about this; just know what
base you're supposed to cover in any given situation:

• *Runner on first, base hit—you back up third base.*
• *Runner on second, base hit—you back up home plate.*
• *Two runners on, base hit—you follow the ball and back up wherever the
throw is heading:* You follow the ball; the goal is to be in the right place at the
right time to handle an errant overthrow of a base. This is a commonsense kind
of deal. I've seen Maddux and Smoltz catch overthrows on the fly behind home
plate. Smoltz is a tremendous athlete, and he always knows where to go to back
up the right base.

Pickoff plays: On the pickoff to second base we believe in the daylight play—
the shortstop sneaks in behind the runner, who is taking his lead, breaks
toward second, and the pitcher turns and throws to the bag. That's the only
play we have. Why try to memorize a million plays when one of them—execut-
ed properly—does the job?

This is is just like our philosophy of pitching: Command of your fastball and
change speeds. Keep it simple.

The Atlanta Braves don't have any trick plays, and personally, I don't believe in them.

Now, when we talk about the pickoff play at first, the simple truth is that you're not going to pick off many runners. When you're holding runners on at first or second you're trying to keep them from taking the extra base.

These days pitchers go to a slide-step (when you come set to your stretch position you unload quickly to the plate; you never lift your leg, just stride out and deliver the pitch) to minimize the time it takes to get the pitch to home plate. The thinking behind this technique is that it helps the catcher throw a runner out who is trying to steal the base.

But, quite frankly, some pitchers can do it and some can't. You have to break your hands quickly out of the glove. When you slide-step you'd better have the ball out of your glove quickly—out, up, and in that cocked position we talked about in chapter 3—to ensure that your upper body doesn't lag behind your lower body on the delivery. The consequence of messing this up is getting *underneath the ball,* a sure way to throw a bad pitch, and that runner you are trying so hard to hold on is probably going to score.

Next thing you know, you'll be backing up third base—another one of those PFP drills Neagle told you about.

When you are holding a runner on—and this is true for all pitchers—your top priority is to throw a quality pitch and retire the hitter. Remember what I told you earlier on—one run in an inning will rarely kill you.

It's when the floodgates open and three or four runs score in an inning that you're out of the game; those big innings are often the product of a pitcher paying so much attention to the runner that he forgets what he is out there to do in the first place.

A quick release on the pitch is the most effective way to hold a runner on and keep him close to the bag. Throwing over to the first baseman time after time after time is a joke. The slide-step eliminates all the nonsense of throwing over too much.

You can be just as effective with a slide-step or pitching out of the stretch, but I don't like to see a pitcher start an inning out of the stretch if there's no one on base. I believe in a full delivery, a full windup, because there's more deception.

And deception is one of the five weapons in your arsenal: stuff, location, movement, change of speeds, and deception.

Let me tell you something Greg Maddux preaches about holding runners on before we move on to physical conditioning for pitchers:

> I don't care if the guy runs on me. A guy can reach first and I'll get one out. He can steal second and I'll get a second out. He can move up one more base, but I'll get that third out before he scores.

Maddux may not be like you or me, but that mentality of complete self-confidence is what I want you take to the mound every time you pitch.

Chapter 6
Physical Conditioning for Pitchers

The history of strength training for pitching is filled with controversy and—to a great extent—misunderstanding. The baseball establishment has—until very recently—been less than enthusiastic about pitchers lifting weights for fear that arm injuries would ensue.

This fear has been minimized with the help of the efforts of Nolan Ryan and a select few pitchers and coaches who have proven that intelligent training can often prevent the elbow and shoulder injuries that plague pitchers.

To complement the throwing program outlined by Leo Mazzone, here are Frank Fultz's (the Braves' strength coach's) comments on how he structures the training regimen for pitchers.

—Jim Rosenthal

My objective is to implement a day-in, day-out conditioning regimen that pitchers can use to add strength, flexibility, and cardiovascular fitness.

I've been lucky enough to work with great pitching coaches such as Leo Mazzone, Les Moss, and Ray Miller. Each of these pitching gurus has impressed upon me the importance of range of motion within the shoulder joint, without overdevelopment of the shoulder muscles.

I had the pleasure of seeing this principle put into play by Nolan Ryan when I worked for the Houston Astros in the eighties. Nolan would train hard, but not to the point where he limited his flexibility or where he gained any substantive muscle size. The goal is to build functional strength, for both the upper and lower body, that will help you as a pitcher.

Weight training is vital for pitchers. As a young athlete you need to strengthen the back, shoulders, and legs to maximize your potential. Strength training begins in high school; Little League pitchers have no reason to worry about anything besides just learning how to play the game the right way and to enjoy it thoroughly.

The objective is to get stronger—not bigger. Our pitchers with the Braves have followed the basic program carefully and consistently. It's one of the many training tools that have allowed them to stay healthy and strong from one season to the next.

I'm going to outline the in-season conditioning program for Braves pitchers to get you on the right track with your own program: lower-body training, upper-body training, cardiovascular (or aerobic) exercise, and the 7–4–7 program (with either light dumbbells or weighted baseballs) for the health of the shoulders and elbows.

Tom Glavine is an excellent role model for any young pitcher. He prepares himself for his skill by both throwing on the side with Leo Mazzone and working with me in the weight room, every day. Glavine's work ethic is superb; his attitude is exemplary.

The Schedule*

Monday
- Glavine pitches.

Tuesday and Thursday
- Glavine reports to the weight room and hits both upper and lower body in one training session. Always start with lower-body training to deal with the fatigue factor.

Lower-Body Training Objectives
The leg press, or leg slide, closely replicates the physical requirements of the back leg during the pitching delivery. That's why the leg press is the core strength exercise in the program.

The Format Glavine will do three sets of 12 repetitions of the first four exercises, going up in weight with each set. On the fifth exercise—leg presses—he'll do five sets of 12 reps to shock the muscle with resistance and, again, he will add weight with each set. All exercises are performed on machines to ensure safety.

The Exercises
(1) Leg extensions (quadriceps—thighs)
(2) Leg curls (hamstrings)
(3) Adduction/abduction machine (groin)
(4) Calf raises (calves)
(5) Leg presses (quads/overall leg strength)

---

*A note on relief pitchers: Obviously, our relievers don't have the ability to predict when—or how often—they will pitch in a game; therefore, they do the 7–4–7 program after the game and the upper-and-lower-body training regimen three days per week (Monday, Wednesday, and Friday) when we're at home. On the road it's less scientific, but we make sure they get their lifting in.

Upper-Body Training Objectives

Number one: to increase strength but not to limit flexibility or add any substantive muscle size. Number two: to fatigue the muscles the day after pitching. The key with upper-body lifting for pitchers is to limit the weight (they lift just enough weight to complete 15 or 25 precise repetitions) and to do all the exercises on machines to ensure stability and safety. So, unlike lower-body training, do not go up in weight on each set; select a weight and stick with it for the entire workout.

The Format Glavine will do three exercises—one each for chest, back, and shoulders—for two sets of 15 reps. Then he'll select three different machines to target the same body parts but only do one set of 25 reps for each. He'll finish with two sets of 15 reps for biceps and triceps, one exercise per body part.

The Exercises

Phase 1:
- Smith machine bench presses with narrow grip (chest)
- Back presses on lat pull-down machine (back)
- Shoulder presses (shoulders)

Phase 2:
- Machine bench presses (chest)
- Back presses (back)
- Lateral raises (shoulders)

Phase 3:
- Biceps curls (biceps)
- Triceps pushdowns (triceps)

Tuesday–Thursday: Treadmill Training

- Tuesday: Glavine does 20 minutes on the treadmill at 7 mph.
- Wednesday: He'll do a sprint workout—30 seconds on, 15 seconds off (the

treadmill), 30 seconds on, 15 seconds off; this format duplicates the aerobic-training benefits of doing wind sprints.

•Thursday: Interval training, which is five minutes of distance and one-minute intervals with different speed settings on the treadmill.

Tuesday–Friday

•Glavine uses the 7–4–7 program to prevent shoulder, elbow, and wrist injuries. You can do this program either with weighted baseballs—three- or five-pounders—or with very light dumbbells, 2.5 pounds on the low end and five pounds on the high end.

Objectives

This is a comprehensive training program designed to fatigue the muscles of the upper body—shoulders in particular—that are associated with throwing a baseball. Done properly, these exercises will help to lower the risk of elbow and shoulder injuries.

Glavine favors the weighted balls; Maddux prefers the dumbbells. I've included photos of both Maddux and Glavine to give you an idea of what these exercises look like in either variation.

The first seven are done standing; the middle four are done seated over a bench; the final seven are performed lying down on a table. Perform one set of 15 repetitions of each exercise.

Exercise List

Standing:

(1) Front shoulder raise

(2) Side shoulder raise

(3) Turned-in shoulder raise—the movement is comparable to emptying a can of soda

(4) Bend at the waist and do a back shoulder raise (or flye)

(5) Triceps kickback

(6) Biceps curl

(7) Shoulder shrug

Seated:

(1) Front wrist curl

(2) Back wrist curl

(3) Slider wrist curl—turning your wrist as if you were throwing a breaking ball

(4) Wrist rollover

Lying on bench:

(1) Side shoulder raise

(2) Lying back arm raise

(3) Abbreviated back shoulder raise

(4) *L*-shaped arm raise/reverse *L*-shaped arm raise

(5) External shoulder rotation

(6) Triceps push out

(7) Internal shoulder rotation

Saturday:

Glavine makes his next start and he's ready to go.

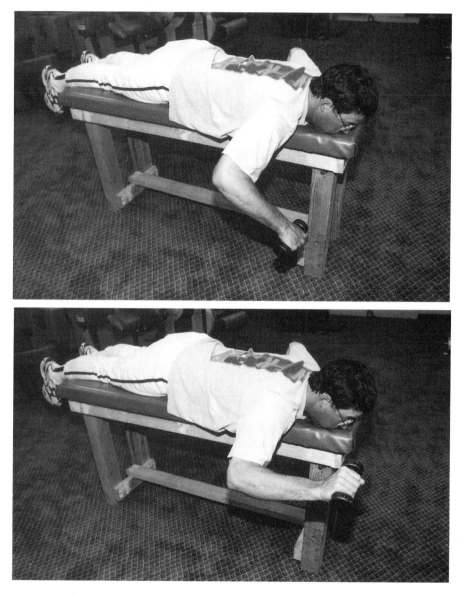

1–2 • Greg Maddux Sequence: L-shaped arm raise: Raise throwing hand in
L-shaped position until it's parallel (at a right angle) to the top of the bench.

3•Turned-in shoulder raise: Start dumbbell at thigh level and raise it to shoulder height. The position of the dumbbell should look as if you are emptying a can of Coke.

4•Side shoulder raise: Lift dumbbell from hip level to shoulder height.

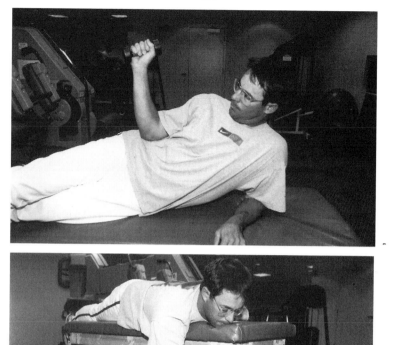

5•External shoulder rotation: Start dumbbell at mid-line of body and raise to oblique—from parallel to floor position to perpendicular.

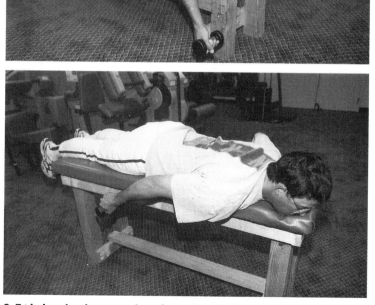

6–7•Lying back arm raise: Start dumbbell at perpendicular-to-floor position and raise to parallel.

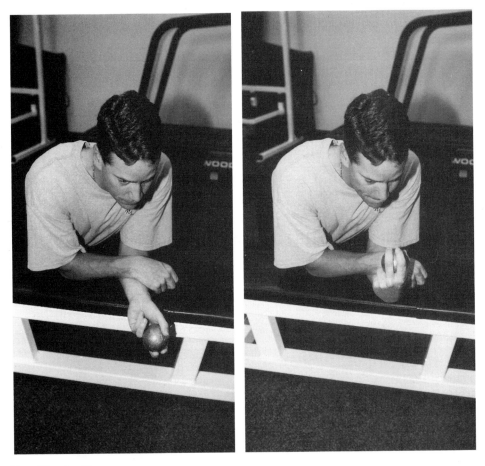

Tom Glavine Sequence:

8–9•Front wrist curl: Wrist extension to wrist flexion. Curl wrist to bring weighted baseball from below to above bench level. Nonworking arm rests across throwing arm for support.

10–11•Triceps kickback: Kick the weighted ball back—straightening the elbow as you go.

12 • **Biceps curl:** Curl the balls up until the arms are bent at the elbow; contract your biceps at the top—lift only as high as range of motion will allow.

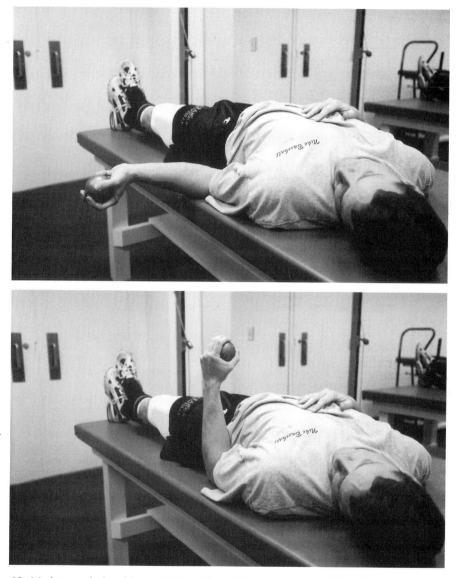

13–14 • Internal shoulder rotation: Start with your arm parallel to the floor, and as you raise the weighted ball the arm becomes perpendicular.

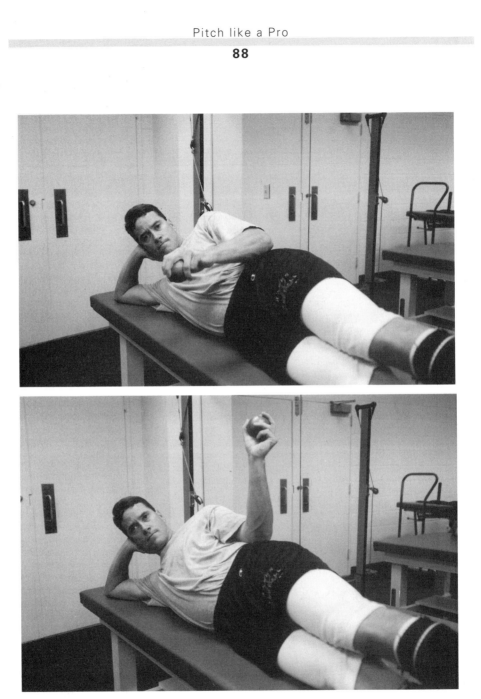

15–16 • External shoulder rotation: Reverse the angle of the internal rotation; raise ball from parallel to perpendicular.

Chapter 7
Mazzone's Musings

About once a generation you get a pitching coach with the talent and insight of a Leo Mazzone. Along with former hitting instructor Clarence Jones and the rest of the Braves coaching staff, Mazzone has given manager Bobby Cox a mix of experience, wisdom, and innovation.

In this final chapter, we bring you the wit and wisdom of Mazzone as he tackles a variety of baseball issues and personalities.

—Jim Rosenthal

On Relief Pitching

It used to be they made you a relief pitcher if you weren't good enough to be a starter. Those days are gone, what with the specialization of relief pitching and all the importance it is given in baseball today. But I believe that if you're a top prospect you should be a starting pitcher during your developmental phase—right through from college into A, AA, and AAA baseball. This way you know exactly what pitches you have in your repertoire and how to use them effectively.

You often hear about a young fastball pitcher being converted into a closer in college or A ball. What's the point in that? It means that for his entire career he'll fire away with blind heat—throw practically nothing but fastballs—and he won't learn anything about pitching.

The most important thing a pitcher can do to improve his pitches is accumulate a lot of innings. Suffice it to say, it's very difficult to accumulate innings—and improve the quality of your pitches—when you're working out of the bullpen as a youngster.

I don't think pitching 50 or 60 innings a year—when you're trying to make it to the big leagues—is going to cut it.

I'll give you an example of what I'm talking about. Steve Bedrosian had the best fastball of any pitcher I've ever coached. It was a killer fastball—and I don't care what it registered on the radar gun. It was in the nineties and had all sorts of movement. He had the best arm of any pitcher I've worked with in my entire coaching career.

Despite the fact that he was a great relief pitcher at the major league level, Bedrosian was used strictly as a starting pitcher in the minor leagues. He accumulated a lot of innings. He fanned a lot of hitters. He learned a lot about pitching and how to make quality pitches under pressure. He never pitched a single inning of relief in the minor leagues!

Steve Bedrosian won the Cy Young Award with the Philadelphia Phillies as the premier closer in baseball in 1987. He was one of the best relievers in the history of the National League. And yet he learned how to pitch as a starter. In my book, that is how you prepare your great closers for success.

On Being a One-Pitch Pitcher

Steve Avery was the Dodger killer on our staff in 1991—the greatest year I've ever spent in my baseball career—and he's a good example of how a young pitcher must resist the temptation to rely strictly on the fastball.

Avery signed as a power pitcher out of high school in Michigan and cruised through the minor leagues, dominating hitters at every level.

Then he struggled when he first got to the major leagues, as young pitchers tend to do. But in 1991 he had a great season, and one of the reasons for that success was that he trusted in his ability to throw the breaking ball and the change-up for strikes. This is no small accomplishment, as power pitchers face a lot of pressure from minor league managers to only throw the fastball in crucial situations.

You run into a spot where you throw the change to a hitter with men on base and the guy hits a home run. Remember when Mark Wohlers was crucified by the media for throwing a slider to Jim Leyritz in the '96 World Series? But you have to be able to trust in your off-speed pitches. And this gets back to the fact that you can't survive—quite often even in Little League—as a one-pitch pitcher.

If you can't change speeds, what happens?

You have to overexert and overextend your arm.

What does overextension lead to?

An increased risk of arm injuries.

It's a vicious cycle, but one that can be avoided if you learn how to throw quality pitches.

On Don Drysdale

He told me that the Braves' staff in the nineties reminded him of the great Dodger pitching staffs with Koufax in the sixties. That's one of the nicest compliments our pitching staff has ever gotten from anyone in baseball.

On Structuring a Pitching Staff

You must have six or seven pitchers doing the bulk of the work on a pitching staff. If you have all 11 guys getting the call on a regular basis, it probably means that your starting pitchers are struggling.

Some people will tell you that all 11 of your pitchers must get into games on a regular basis, but I don't agree; frankly, I hope we go through a season where some of them don't get any work in games. But one way or the other, thanks to the throwing program, they'll all be ready to pitch when we need them.

On the Need for Running Drills for Pitchers

Our credo with the Braves is that we throw a lot and we run a little. Baseball is a game of starting and stopping—that's why sprinting is much more useful than distance work for pitchers.

The program in spring training is to run 10 wind sprints—from the foul line to center field—and to add two per day until the guys are running 20 sprints per session. I don't believe in counting each sprint, but I will watch to see who is working hard and who is loafing. Most of our pitchers are hard workers, so I don't have to look over their shoulders. This will vary from one pitching staff to the next.

Our goal is to bring a pitcher's legs along slowly—just as we bring the arm along slowly—in spring training. Why kill them with running drills? The object is to make a pitcher feel better physically, not worse.

On Coaching the Braves' Pitching Staff

Tom Glavine has a thick skin, so he can handle some very honest dialogue about pitching. He and I have had some fun arguments through the years.

John Smoltz can get a little emotional, but he's come a long way in that area. And, of course, he's a perfectionist, which is true of all our starting pitchers.

Denny Neagle is the funniest guy you'd ever want to meet—except on the day he's going to pitch and then you can hardly speak to him.

Greg Maddux, whom we call Mad Dog, is the one who is thinking all the time, trying to figure everything out.

Maddux asked me a question based on a hypothetical situation that could arise in the play-offs against the Cincinnati Reds back in 1995. Here's the situation: It's the seventh inning. There's a runner on second base who represents the tying or winning run.

Maddux asked me: "Who do you want me to pitch to—Reggie Sanders or Willie Green?"

I told him Willie Green—with no hesitation.

I explained my reasoning: Reggie Sanders is a guy who strikes out against pitchers who throw north and south—baseball lingo for up and down. But Maddux is more of an east and west pitcher—inside and outside.

Willie Green? I know for a fact that he can't hit Maddux's change-up.

Maddux looked at me and said, "You're right!"

A coach can't be 50–50 in dealing with pitchers. The pitchers want an honest answer when they ask a question.

On Coaching Young Pitchers

The objective is to coach with energy, enthusiasm, and compassion. This applies to the young pitcher who tends to be very emotional; it applies to a coach in understanding the personality of the players, knowing what tone of voice to use.

Emotions play a big part in how a pitch is going to be thrown, and this is as true for Little League pitchers as it is for veteran major leaguers.

On Whitey Ford and Johnny Sain

When Johnny Sain took over as the Yankees' pitching coach, the book on Whitey Ford was that he was too small to handle the wear and tear of a four-man rotation.

Sain got his hands on Ford, implemented a throwing program, and Whitey went from 12–9 in 1960 (193 innings) to 25–4 in 1961 (284 innings, to lead the American League). Good coaching can make a big difference; the key is to believe in your pitchers and to give them what they need—mentally and physically—to get the most out of their skills and potential.

On David Cone

One of the nicest compliments I've ever received was from David Cone at the 1997 All-Star Game. He walked up to me before the game and said, "I really appreciate the fact that you are with your pitchers 100 percent of the time on every pitch they throw. My only regret in my baseball career is that I never got to pitch for you."

As a pitching coach I'm not going to chart every pitch and write it down; I watch my pitcher—his mound presence, his facial expressions—and how he's unloading the pitches will tell me more than anything I can mark down on a piece of paper.

You can't take the human element out of coaching or you miss the many pleasures of learning, improving, and winning.

On Pitching Inside

Even with all the success we've had with our pitching staff in Atlanta, we still get criticized—by the so-called experts—for not pitching inside enough. As Tom Glavine said: "What the hell; isn't anyone watching our games?"

We will pitch inside, but we believe in doing it selectively.

The Braves' pitchers always have the lowest number of hit batsmen every year. Do you know why? Because that macho garbage of pitching inside is reserved for mediocre staffs. They're giving up a bunch of runs, get upset, and start drilling people.

We win quietly—bang, bang, bang—and it's, See you later.